Presented To:

_____

From:

_____

Date:

_____

In Pursuit of Wholeness

In Pursuit of Wholeness

Experiencing God's Salvation for the Total Person

WILFRED GRAVES JR., PH.D.

DESTINY IMAGE® PUBLISHERS, INC.

P.O. Box 310, Shippensburg, PA 17257-0310

"Speaking to the Purposes of God for This Generation and for the Generations to Come."

This book and all other Destiny Image, Revival Press, MercyPlace, Fresh Bread, Destiny Image Fiction, and Treasure House books are available at Christian bookstores and distributors worldwide.

For a U.S. bookstore nearest you, call 1-800-722-6774
For more information on foreign distributors, call 717-532-3040.
Reach us on the Internet: www.destinyimage.com.

ISBN 13 TP: 978-0-7684-3794-2
ISBN 13 HC: 978-0-7684-3795-9
ISBN 13 LP: 978-0-7684-3796-6
ISBN 13 E-book: 978-0-7684-8991-0

For Worldwide Distribution, Printed in the U.S.A.
1 2 3 4 5 6 7 8 9 10 / 15 14 13 12 11

Dedication

To my parents, with love.

Acknowledgments

I began seriously to examine the issues of salvation and wholeness while a master of divinity student. The classes of Peter Wagner, Siang-Yang Tan, Charles Kraft, and other professors at Fuller Theological Seminary introduced me to the concepts of physical healing, emotional healing, and deliverance as aspects of God's salvation for humankind. In those days, I also encountered the works of Francis MacNutt, Ken Blue, Leanne Payne, Ed Murphy, and several other writers that further challenged me to reflect on God's salvific remedy for humanity's spiritual, mental, physical, and social ills. In my systematic theology courses with David Dorman and Miroslav Volf, I learned that salvation broadly defined is God's process of bringing all things into conformity with His divine plans and purposes. Salvation, then, includes more than gaining entry into Heaven; it involves the continual rescue of persons from sin and its effects until the consummation of all things in Jesus Christ.

At West Angeles Church of God in Christ, where I currently serve on the ministry staff, people often experience transformation through evangelical conversion, physical or emotional healing, release from substance abuse, or economic empowerment. Ministry within the urban context of Los Angeles, California, has afforded me numerous opportunities to see the awesome power of God at work in the salvation and restoration of shattered lives. I thank all who have inspired this book through their teachings, writings, or experiences.

I must recognize a few individuals specifically for their vital contributions to the finalization of this book. Tracy Williams, my aunt, offered valuable editorial advice. Drs. Rick and Patty Williamson reviewed the entire manuscript and gave me many helpful suggestions from both a biblical and psychological perspective. Glendolyn Graves, my mother, gave me thoughtful, creative feedback as well. Uleses Henderson and Deborah Pegues helped me to review the publishing agreement. Wilmer Singleton and the team at Destiny Image Publishers worked diligently to position the book for marketing success.

Many family members and friends encouraged me throughout the writing process. A special word of thanks goes to my dear friends Hans and Swann Van Delden, Dwight and Rachelle Thompson, Ron Mariani, and Leslie Forbes-Mariani, who have supported my personal and professional endeavors in countless ways. I also recognize the following individuals for their prayers, advice, words of wisdom, and/or assistance with this project: Lula Ballton, Charletta Benjamin, Charles Blake II, Larry Blake, James Bradley, Anasa Briggs-Graves, Dennis Bullock, Anton Burrell, Ivan Cole, Nettie Cole, Lauren Corley, Lana Duim, Yvonne Gibson-Johnson, Timothy Godfrey, Marion Green, Kenneth Hammonds, Aaron Howard, Diane Jasperson, Collette Johnson, Earl Jordan, Victor Joseph, Paul Lewis, Nolanda Love, Bryan McGinley, David McNeil, Oscar Owens, Edwin Petrossi, Sylvia Reid, Gladys Ross, Klaus and Carole Schiessel, Sonja Sharp, Benjamin and Mary Smith, James Smith, Benjamin and Latonya Stephens, Albert Tevanyan, Manuel Thomas, Robert Turner, and Robert and Adetayo West.

The members of the "Prayer Sisters" Bible study class have been continual sources of inspiration and encouragement. Thank you, Akosua Busia, Andi Chapman, LaTanya Richardson Jackson, Cookie Johnson, Pat Kelly, Jennifer McHenry, Candida

Mobley-Wright, Pat Moore, Eula Smith, Cheri Townsend, and Charlayne Woodard.

I thank my pastor, Bishop Charles E. Blake Sr., for his significant contribution to my spiritual growth and ministerial development. His wife, Mae L. Blake, also has spoken positive words into my life on numerous occasions. Finally, I thank my parents, Wilfred Graves Sr. and Glendolyn K. Graves, for their love, nurture, and constant support. I dedicate this work to them.

Endorsements

I strongly commend Dr. Graves for this excellent work and for his continued dedication to the practical application of God's Word in the power of the Holy Spirit. *In Pursuit of Wholeness* will help countless people to experience the fullness of God's salvation for the total person. I pray that the book blesses your life and that you will never be the same again.

Charles E. Blake Sr.
Presiding Bishop, Church of God in Christ
Pastor, West Angeles Church of God in Christ

Wilfred Graves Jr. is a trusted and proven servant with a distinct heart of wisdom and grace for helping people needing Christ's liberating touch to heal every aspect of our lives. In this helpful book, Dr. Graves presents simple, yet illuminating, strategies for clear and definite steps to wholeness in Christ and personal transformation. This book will change your life if you take its principles to heart.

Jack W. Hayford
Chancellor, The King's University
Founding Pastor, The Church On The Way
Los Angeles, California

The times we live in require special coping tools to inspire us to keep going and move forward. Dr. Wilfred Graves Jr. leads us through the teachings of the Bible and uncovers powerful principles to uplift us and give us access to sustainable encouragement. He truly gives us God's ideas.

LaTanya Richardson Jackson
Actress, Philanthropist

Dr. Wilfred Graves Jr. is a great thinker and wonderful teacher. He communicates truth in ways that are both profound and easy to understand. People from all walks of life will find peace, wholeness, and personal transformation in the pages of this phenomenal volume. This is one book that you will want to read from cover to cover.

Cookie Johnson
Entrepreneur, Philanthropist
Secretary, Magic Johnson Foundation Board of Directors

Dr. Graves is concerned, as we all should be, that all Christ's followers experience the more abundant life that Jesus has promised us (see John 10:10). Unfortunately, many people miss that abundance. They may be wonderfully saved, but their Christian experience falls short of what they pray for. As Dr. Graves says, "This book is for those seeking to experience the fullness of God's salvation in their individual lives."

Though we are promised this abundant life as a part of our salvation, for many, perhaps for most who find it, abundance is a second step. And for those who don't find it, it is but a dream. God wants us to be free and alive in Him. But He requires that we cooperate with Him to bring His will about. A major focus of the book is on what we need to do to work with God to experience this aliveness. This is a book to help us become what both God and we ourselves want us to be.

Charles H. Kraft
Senior Professor of Anthropology and Intercultural
Communication, Fuller Theological Seminary

I heartily endorse Dr. Graves' encouraging—and life-changing—teaching that God wants not just to heal physical sickness but also to heal the brokenness of our lives while on earth. There is hardly a day that goes by when I don't *see* it usually happening in someone's life.

Francis MacNutt, Ph.D.
Co-Founder, Christian Healing Ministries, Inc.
Jacksonville, Florida

Dr. Wilfred Graves' volume, *In Pursuit of Wholeness,* is a very significant book. As a pastor, he has seen his share of those in need of salvation and those in need of wholeness. As a scholar, he has thought about these themes both long and carefully. Rarely does a book on salvation or wholeness achieve what Dr. Graves has achieved in this book. He has brought these thoughts together in a compelling narrative. His reflections are rich and well worth pondering by mature Christians. Yet his language and illustrations are simple enough to make sense and to provide sound answers to the questions that many people in our day are asking. They come from real life, and as such, they provide real solutions to daily problems. This is a book full of wisdom that is born of God and rooted in everyday life. It is sound and practical. I found it to be a masterpiece of practical, pastoral theology, and I am honored to be able to recommend it to you.

Cecil M. Robeck Jr.
Professor of Church History and Ecumenics
Fuller Theological Seminary

I have known Wilfred Graves Jr. for nearly 20 years. He is a dynamic teacher and preacher who correctly handles the Word of God and possesses a genuine love and compassion for people. *In Pursuit of Wholeness* is a comprehensive guide to spiritual, mental, and physical well-being through the appropriation of the Gospel's timeless message of salvation. I enjoyed reading it immensely, and I know that it will be a blessing to many.

Paul Thomas
Lead Pastor, Evangel Temple Assembly of God
Columbus, Georgia

Some people think that "salvation" means being born again and going to Heaven. Yes, that is true, but when you read *In Pursuit of Wholeness* you will discover that salvation is much, much more. Wilfred Graves takes you on a journey that will enrich your life here on earth as well as someday in Heaven. You need this book to fulfill the wonderful destiny that God has for your life.

C. Peter Wagner,
Apostolic Ambassador Global Spheres, Inc.

Contents

Foreword

The good news of the Gospel is that Jesus Christ came to save broken humanity. He came to restore our shattered relationship with the Father and to minister wholeness to our lives. God's salvation includes provisions for our spirits, minds, emotions, bodies, relationships, finances, etc. Although we await a glorious life in Heaven that will be completely free from sin, sickness, pain, and death, we actually can enjoy the firstfruits of eternal life right now while we presently are on earth. The Lord wants to liberate us from sin and the dire consequences that ensue from spiritual separation from Him. He calls us to submit our lives to Him and to accept His divine path to healing and restoration. He offers salvation, abundant life, and well-being for the total person.

I currently pastor a church with a clear mission to evangelize, edify, and equip the entire person. Through our various ministries and outreach efforts, we touch the lives of literally thousands of people and help them to mature in their personal relationship with God, to serve others, to grow individually, and to become worshipers in spirit and in truth. As the Presiding Bishop of one of the country's largest denominations, I have a unique perspective on many of the key issues now affecting the nation and the world. I believe that the message of salvation through Jesus Christ has never been more pertinent than it is today. The modern world desperately needs a fresh introduction to the Savior.

Dr. Wilfred Graves Jr. shares my passion to reach hurting people. In this timely book, he communicates to the Body of Christ
essential biblical principles related to the themes of salvation and
wholeness. I believe that his insights will inspire you to develop
greater trust and expectation as you look to the Lord to mend
the broken areas of your life. I strongly commend Dr. Graves for
this excellent work and for his continued dedication to the practical application of God's Word in the power of the Holy Spirit.
In Pursuit of Wholeness will help countless people to experience
the fullness of God's salvation for the total person. I pray that the
book blesses your life and that you will never be the same again.

Bishop Charles E. Blake Sr.
Presiding Bishop, Church of God in Christ
Pastor, West Angeles Church of God in Christ
Founder and CEO, Save Africa's Children
Founder, West Angeles Community Development Corporation

Preface

Wednesday afternoon finally arrived. A dear friend and his wife had invited me to a pre-Thanksgiving dinner party, and I was quite eager to sample the hors d'oeuvres. While at the gathering, I met a wealthy executive in his mid-70s named Ernest. Ernest, who was a devout Catholic, told me that he actually could see the joy of the Lord on me as I entered the room, and that he wanted to experience that same joy for himself. As I talked with Ernest for several minutes, he began to share with me that he longed for a profound encounter with God. He said that he admired Billy Graham and the evangelical wing of Christianity because of the well-defined conversion experience of its members. Ernest liked the notion of an altar call and a public declaration of faith in Jesus Christ. He sincerely desired to know God more deeply. Although he was a professing Christian, he longed for a personal relationship with the Lord that was more intimate and more satisfying. Ernest needed a fresh introduction to the Savior.

Michelle also needed to experience the Savior's power. One Sunday evening after church, she asked me for an appointment to discuss several issues of importance to her. The urgency in her voice deeply concerned me, so I agreed to meet with her. When Michelle came to my office later in the week, she was depressed, distraught, and full of fear. As tears streamed down her face, she told me that she was in great physical pain and that the enemy seemed to be harassing her in every area of life. She truly loved the Lord and was quite open to whatever wisdom He was willing to

21

impart to her. "I need God right now," she exclaimed. "I feel like I'm losing my mind!" My heart went out to Michelle as we went before the Lord in prayer.

My own dear mother, Glendolyn, is no stranger to suffering. She experienced the death of a baby through miscarriage. She became a single parent in her mid-30s, and around the same time, she endured various health challenges, including pneumonia, hypertension, congestive heart failure, and renal failure. During the last few years, my mother has spent numerous hours in hospital rooms and has fought off death on more than one occasion. Currently, she is a dialysis patient and bears every physical challenge with poise and dignity. Throughout her life, she sometimes has faced bewilderment and discouragement, but she joyfully testifies that God has extended His grace to her in the midst of her most difficult trials. "I have learned that God is never far away," she says. "He's a very present help in times of trouble."

Yet, what does God offer to Ernest, Michelle, and Glendolyn to help them with their troubles? How can they have a greater awareness of God's presence and a fuller experience of His power? Are there some resources from which they can draw to bring them to a state of wholeness and well-being? I believe that God's response to humanity's spiritual, mental, physical, and other types of brokenness is salvation. This book examines salvation and several ways in which we can experience its benefits more fully.

Salvation is a fascinating subject. Taken in a positive sense, salvation indicates a state of well-being or wholeness. The term also expresses the notion of deliverance from harm or rescue from danger. Jesus Christ came to save humanity from sin and its effects.[1] He came to destroy the works of the devil, to deliver us from God's wrath, and to give eternal life to everyone who will believe in Him (see 1 John 3:8; Eph. 2:3; John 3:16-17). For the past 12 years or so, I have studied salvation and taught extensively on the topic in my church, in Bible college courses, and in other Christian settings. The theme also has been consistent in much of my preaching for nearly a decade. Each decision for Christ following a sermon gives me immense joy and tremendous satisfaction. It is a rewarding yet humbling task to deliver a message of reconciliation and hope to people. I have come to understand by experience that the Gospel really is "good news" to lost individuals.

On the morning of Wednesday, June 27, 2007, I awakened with a strong impression to write a book about salvation and its implications, entitled *In Pursuit of Wholeness: Experiencing God's Salvation for the Total Person.* I am convinced that God plans not just to offer people entry into Heaven, but also to heal the brokenness in their lives while on earth. God's salvation extends to the entire human person: spirit, mind, and body. Jesus Christ frequently healed the sick and cast out demons, revealing a holistic concern for others. There often are times during ministry today when physical healing, deliverance, or even miracles accompany the preaching of the Gospel. God wants to bring wholeness to our lives.

This overwhelming truth about God's intent gripped my heart strongly on that Wednesday morning. God seemed to be prompting me to organize the vast amount of teaching material on salvation that I had amassed. I knew that it definitely was time for me to put my thoughts and writings into readable form. I began to enter my impressions into my daily prayer journal, and within a few minutes, I had a workable outline for the present manuscript.

Wholeness is something I desire for myself. During daily times of prayer and meditation on Scripture, the Savior often challenges me to surrender to Him the broken areas of my life that need repair. The Lord graciously heals and restores me continually as I seek Him on a consistent basis. God does not always remove the challenges I face, but He sustains me every day and gives me strength to endure each difficulty.

This book is for those seeking to experience the fullness of God's salvation in their individual lives. Among the men and women reading this book, there will be a broad spectrum of age groups, backgrounds, ability levels, and life experiences. Some of you are seasoned Christians. Others of you may be only now beginning your spiritual walk. All of us, no matter how long we have been serving the Lord, truly need His strength to survive the challenges of life.

So many people are hurting today (spiritually, emotionally, physically, and relationally) and need God's gracious offer of healing and restoration. Perhaps you are experiencing grief, having financial troubles, suffering with an illness, or dealing with other serious problems. Sometimes life's difficulties can overwhelm us and rob us of peace and joy. Maybe you are not facing a crisis right now, but perhaps a loved one is currently going through a major challenge. God has not forgotten your struggles or those of countless other hurting people. He wants to reveal Himself in special ways, even in the midst of trying circumstances. I believe that this work will be a source of comfort and hope to you and will help to increase your awareness of God's love and power. It is my prayer that you will benefit from the book and that you will soon come to experience the fullness of God's salvation in your personal pursuit of wholeness.

In Pursuit of Wholeness

The man at the pool of Bethesda had suffered 38 years with an infirmity. When Jesus sees the state of the man, He asks him an important question, "Do you want to be made whole?" (see John 5:5-6). The man desires physical healing and receives it from the Great Physician. Later in the story, Jesus encounters the man in the temple and says to him, "See, you have been made whole. Do not sin anymore, so that nothing worse happens to you" (see John 5:14). Jesus exhibits concern for the man's physical and spiritual well-being and cures him of his brokenness. The Savior now offers wholeness to everyone who will receive it from Him in faith. His question to us is the same as to the man at the pool of Bethesda: "Do you want to be made whole?"

Wholeness is healthiness in every area of life. We all desire it. Yet, is it possible to experience? We live in a broken world, and many of us lead very broken lives. Some are on a path of sin and personal destruction. Sin alienates us from God, who alone is the very source of life, salvation, and wholeness. Others are plagued by fear, violence, addiction, or disease. Still others face vicious cycles of poverty, pain, oppression, and despair. What can be done about all this? What is God's will concerning human brokenness? What resources does He provide to help us amid the difficulties and tragedies of life? What is the divine pathway to wholeness?

This book explores the benefits of salvation for the total person. God's salvation, which He offers to humanity through Jesus Christ, includes provisions for the spirit, mind, and body. It involves the healing of relationships and the transformation of society. Salvation is a process of restoration and renewal of all things to God's original intent. Salvation, then, has meaning for all aspects of the Christian life.

I write from an evangelical and a Pentecostal perspective. I believe that God eternally exists as Father, Son, and Holy Spirit and that each person of the Trinity is fully God. I embrace the Lordship of Jesus Christ, His atoning sacrifice, His resurrection, His ascension, and every aspect of His person and work that the Scriptures reveal. I believe that the Holy Spirit indwells and empowers believers and applies to them the benefits of salvation that Christ has made freely available to those who put their trust in Him.

This book takes the view that Christians join with God to advance His Kingdom on the earth. God has given us the privilege of helping Him to accomplish His will. It is His will to bring salvation and wholeness to our lives, and we must play a part in receiving His best for us. Salvation is of God and from Him alone; however, there are principles that we must follow from the Bible to enjoy the fullness of the salvation that God extends to us through Christ. Through prayer and fellowshipping with God, through obeying His Word, and through appropriating the resources that He has provided, we can find success in our pursuit of wholeness, and we can enjoy God's best for our lives.

Chapter 1

God: The Source of Life, Security, and Well-being

God is not only infinitely greater and more excellent than all other beings, but He is the head of the universal system of existence; the foundation and fountain of all being and all beauty; from whom all is perfectly derived, and on whom all is most absolutely and perfectly dependent; of whom, and through whom, and to whom is all being and all perfection; and whose being and beauty are, as it were, the sum and comprehension of all existence and excellence: much more than the sun is the fountain and summary comprehension of all the light and brightness of the day.

—Jonathan Edwards[1]

WHO IS THE CHRISTIAN GOD?

The Bible affirms the existence of a Supreme Being called God.[2] Most people believe in God, or at least in a higher power of some kind; however, there are diverse opinions of what God is like. Christianity teaches that God has revealed Himself to us in the Scriptures and that we actually can know Him personally. Although we cannot observe God directly or define Him completely, we can discover many things about Him from the biblical revelation. According to the Bible, God is spirit; He is eternal, self-existent, self-sufficient, and self-sustaining. Theologians use words like omnipotent, omniscient, and omnipresent to describe Him. Morally, He is holy, righteous, gracious, and good. The Bible also describes Him as truth and love, among other noble characteristics. God is perfect and unchanging in His being and character.

The Old and New Testaments reveal that there is one and only one God. For example, Deuteronomy 6:4 reads, *"Hear, O Israel: The Lord our God, the Lord is one."* Similarly, Isaiah 45:5a records the following declaration of the Creator, *"I am the Lord, and there is no other; apart from Me there is no God."* Jesus Christ refers to *"the only true God"* (John 17:3). The apostle Paul also states in First Corinthians 8:6:

> *...there is but one God, the Father, from whom all things came and for whom we live; and there is but one Lord, Jesus Christ, through whom all things came and through whom we live.*

The Bible unequivocally teaches monotheism—the belief in one and only one God. God is the Sovereign Creator and Sustainer of the vast universe in which we live. He alone is the focus of our service and worship. The Bible also reveals that God is three just as He is one. God is Father, Son, and Holy Spirit. The Father is God; the Son is God; and the Holy Spirit is God. The Father, Son, and Holy Spirit are coequal, coeternal, and consubstantial. Theologians speak of a single substance or essence shared by the three members.[3] There are some differences in the roles and functions of these members, but anything that is true of the one God is also true of each of the three members of the Godhead or Trinity.[4]

The Father, Son, and Holy Spirit are not three gods, but rather three persons.[5] They do not differ in their Godhood, only in their personhood. A person is an individual center of rational consciousness. A person thinks, feels, communicates, responds, and is fully self-aware. The opposite of personal is impersonal. A force is impersonal. Energy is impersonal. No member of the Trinity is impersonal. God is not a force; nor is He energy. God is the Creator, the source of life, and the Supreme Ruler of the universe who eternally exists in three persons identified as the Father, Son, and Holy Spirit. A proper understanding of salvation rests upon the solid foundation of the Trinity. God the Father plans or arranges salvation and sends the Son; Jesus Christ accomplishes the Father's plan by dying for the sins of humanity; the Holy Spirit applies the work of Christ to our lives. According to Ephesians 1:3-14, the Father chooses us and accepts us as His children; the Son secures our redemption[6] and the forgiveness of our sins; and the Holy Spirit comes to live within us as a guarantee of our divine inheritance.

The triune God is awesome. In the Old Testament, He reveals to us several names, titles, and descriptions that represent His greatness, His majesty, and His attributes. For example, He is:

- *El Elyon*, the Most High God (see Gen. 14:20; Ps. 78:35);

- *El Shaddai*, the Almighty and All-Sufficient God (see Gen. 17:1; 28:3);

- *Adonai*, the Sovereign Lord and Supreme Ruler (see Gen. 15:2; Ps. 86:12);

- *Yahweh*, I am who I am or I will be who I will be (see Exod. 3:14; 6:3);

- *Yahweh-jireh*, the God who is a Provider (see Gen. 22:14);

- *Yahweh-nissi*, the God who is a Refuge or Banner (see Exod. 17:15);

- *Yahweh-rapha*, the God who is a Healer (see Exod. 15:26);

- *Yahweh-shalom*, the God who is Peace and Well-being (see Judg. 6:24);[7]

- *Yahweh-shammah*, the God who is There (see Ezek. 48:35); and

- *Yahweh-tsidkenu*, the God who is Righteousness (see Jer. 23:5-6).

God is the source of life, peace, well-being, and all that is good. His name represents the fullness of all that He is and everything that He has. Similarly, the name of Jesus represents the totality of His person and work. Even though the name is the translation of a common Palestinian name, *Yeshua*, no one wears the name better than the Son of God. The name Jesus means, "*Yahweh* is Salvation." Salvation includes everything that makes us whole as persons.

I define the term *salvation* as rescue from the things that diminish or destroy us in our spirits, minds, bodies, relationships, and other areas of our humanity. I use the terms *spirit, mind,* and *body* as convenient labels that describe various aspects of human nature; however, there is no strict separation among these three designations. Some things that affect the mind also affect the body. Physical brokenness also can influence the mind and so forth. Human beings are fully integrated units. The Bible values all aspects of our humanity, not just our spirits. Thus, the apostle Paul encourages us to renew our minds (see Rom. 12:2) and declares that our bodies are temples of the Holy Spirit (see 1 Cor. 6:19). The apostle John in the second verse of his third letter writes:

> *Dear friend, I pray that you may enjoy good health and that all may go well with you, even as your soul is getting along well (3 John 2).*

God cares about the total person, and His vision for us is one of wholeness.

Salvation includes not only the forgiveness of sins but also happiness, safety, security, well-being, preservation, protection, victory, and deliverance. The name *Jesus* reminds us that the Son of God truly is the Savior. Even the title "Christ" gives us considerable insight into the ministry of the Lord. The title literally means "Anointed One." Jesus is the Christ, God's special messenger who brings salvation, healing, and deliverance to broken humanity.

The Bible also uses a number of descriptive names of the Holy Spirit. He is Advocate, Comforter, Enabler, Helper, Life-giver, and Teacher. Several metaphors for the Holy Spirit are Breath, Dove, Fire, Oil, Water, and Wind. The Holy Spirit exercises the power of God in creation and redemption. He accomplishes God's work in the Church and manifests the character of Christ in our individual lives. He also equips the Body of Christ to carry out God's ministry of wholeness until the Lord returns. As Christians follow the leading of the Holy Spirit, the Church experiences vitality and growth and becomes more effective in ministry.

STAYING CONNECTED TO GOD

God desires loving fellowship with His people. God created humankind to know Him, and it is His continuing desire that we grow in our relationship with Him. At the very beginning of the Bible in the Book of Genesis before the Fall, Adam and Eve enjoyed unhindered communion with God. They were friends of God. Even after Adam and Eve fell into sin, God did not give up on His creation. He made provision for human salvation and revealed Himself continually to His people.

Throughout the Bible, we find examples of those who sought to maintain their connection to God. Enoch and Noah walked with God, meaning that they pleased God by their lifestyles (see Gen. 5:22-24; Heb. 11:5; Gen. 6:9). Abraham, the father of the faith, also was very close to God. Second Chronicles 20:7 and Isaiah 41:8 both refer to Abraham as a friend of God, indicating that he enjoyed a personal relationship with God. Moses also had a special relationship with God. In fact, Moses had face-to-face conversations with Him (see Deut. 34:10). Psalm 103:7 tells us that God *"made known His ways to Moses, His deeds to the people of Israel."* In other words, Moses understood God more completely than did the children of Israel. The Lord revealed several aspects of His nature to Moses that few others would ever experience.

David was a man who pursued the Lord with passion. In Psalm 63:1, he says that he earnestly seeks God. His soul thirsts for God and his body longs for Him *"in a dry and weary land where there is no water."* In verse 3, David declares, *"Because Your love is better than life, my lips will glorify You."* David was a man after God's own heart (see 1 Sam. 13:14). Although David had flaws and hang-ups, he had a heart that yearned for God. We also need hearts that yearn for the Heavenly Father.

If we genuinely want to understand the concept of fellowship with the Heavenly Father, we should look at the life and teachings of Jesus Christ, our Savior. There is no question that Jesus had a close, personal relationship with His Father. In Matthew 6:5-15 and Luke 11:1-4, Jesus begins His model prayer with the words "Our Father," suggesting intimacy that exists between a parent and child.

In John 4:34, Jesus declares that His food *"is to do the will of Him who sent me and to finish His work."* Hence, Jesus derived total spiritual satisfaction from His relationship with the Father. Doing the Father's will was as natural to Jesus as eating and drinking. In John 5:16-23, Jesus declares that He can do nothing of Himself; He does what He sees the Father doing. Jesus had such a bond with the Heavenly Father that He could say in John 8:29,

"I always do what pleases Him." In the person of Jesus Christ, then, we have the clearest model in all of Scripture of unhindered communion with God.

Not only did Jesus Christ have a special relationship with the Father, but He also makes it possible for us to have a special relationship with God ourselves. Through Christ, we have complete and total access to the Heavenly Father. We have full access to God's presence, power, and provision. It is my prayer that you will come to know God in a close and personal way and that you will experience His salvation and wholeness in every area of your life. Are you ready to receive all that God has for you? Take a moment to worship Him now!

THE RELIABILITY OF GOD IN A CHAOTIC WORLD

One of the major barriers to personal wholeness is the fear of divine abandonment. When the circumstances of life become overwhelming, sometimes the human tendency is to question God's concern, His motives, or even His existence. Yet, the Bible assures us that God loves us and that He cares about our well-being at all times. Psalm 46, in particular, encourages us that He is an ever-present help in times of trouble. When trouble comes into our lives, He is there. When tragedies come into our lives, He is there. When the world seems to be crashing down around us, He is there. When terrorism, war, natural disasters, and calamities begin to spark fear in our hearts, we can take comfort from the reality that God is *with* us and *for* us.

In the first half of verse 1, the psalmist states, *"God is our refuge and strength"* (Ps. 46:1). A refuge is a place of protection, safety, or shelter. It is a place into which to run in order to escape danger. God is our only refuge from ultimate harm. He also is our strength. The word *strength* refers to the notion of security. Therefore, God is our secure refuge or secure protection. He is a stable place of safety where we escape all dangers. The Scriptures declare, *"The name of the Lord is a strong tower; the righteous run to it and are safe"* (Prov. 18:10).

A secure refuge symbolizes salvation. In God are salvation and protection from trouble of every kind. Another translation of refuge is "fortress." Martin Luther wrote a famous hymn based on Psalm 46:1 entitled "A Mighty Fortress Is Our God." Our God is a mighty fortress, a secure refuge, a strong tower, and a stable shelter. God is more than able to keep us safe.

God is also *"an ever-present help in trouble"* (Ps. 46:1). In other words, God has proven that He is reliable. God has so consistently demonstrated His faithfulness in the past that we can trust Him to come through for us in the present. For instance, God did not let you down back in 1981. He worked a miracle for you in 1991. He came through for you again in 2001. Therefore, He is going to be there for you in 2011 and in the future. He is an ever-present help in trouble.

Because God is our refuge and strength, an ever-present help in times of trouble, the first part of verse 2 of Psalm 46 declares, *"Therefore we will not fear."* Fear is faith in reverse. Oftentimes fear causes us to believe things that are untrue. God's Word declares that He is faithful. We say, "God will surely let me down." God's Word declares that He is gracious. We say, "I think that He is holding out on me." God's Word declares that He is love. We say, "I don't think that God really cares about my problems." Fear has no place within the lives of the believers. If we are plagued by fear, then that means that we are not trusting God fully. God is not the source of fear; He is the source of love, power, and soundness of mind, salvation, peace, and wholeness.

The answer to fear is found in verse 7, which reads, *"The Lord Almighty is with us; the God of Jacob is our fortress"* (Ps. 46:7). God does not promise us that we will escape trouble, but He does promise us that He will be with us in the midst of trouble. David declares in Psalm 23:4, *"Even though I walk through the valley of the shadow of death, I will fear no evil, for You are with me."* One day, God will destroy sin, sickness, satan, and death.[8] Until then, His loving presence will sustain us in the midst of adversity.

The King James Version describes God as "The Lord of hosts" *(Yahweh-tsebaoth)* rather than "The Lord Almighty" (NIV) in verses 7 and 11. This name means that heavenly armies surround God. God is a warrior. He is going to fight for us, and He has every available resource to aid, protect, deliver, and comfort us and to ensure our victory against any force that opposes His divine will.

In verse 10, God Himself speaks. He says: *"Be still, and know that I am God; I will be exalted among the nations, I will be exalted in the earth"* (Ps. 46:10).

Here, God is addressing the wicked nations that are fighting against His people. He is saying, "Surrender; put your hands down; stop fighting; you cannot win!" This is what God is saying to our enemies. He is saying, "You cannot win a battle against Me or triumph over My people! I am their strength, their ever-present help, and their total victory! I alone am God, and I am in control!"

We can rejoice over the fact that God is in total control of our lives. We can say with the psalmist in verse 11, *"The Lord Almighty is with us; the God of Jacob is our fortress."* Psalm 46 really is an extended praise to God. The psalm encourages us to magnify the Lord regardless of the circumstances. We can say:

> Even if the earth rips apart, the waters roar, and the mountains are thrown into the sea, I will worship Him. There may be wars, terrorism, calamities, floods, tsunamis, earthquakes, or whatever, but I will worship Him. Trouble is surrounding me on every side, but I will worship and praise the Lord of hosts.

God is *with* us and *for* us, and He is going to help us to endure and to overcome every kind of trouble. I encourage you to put your trust in Him today.

God's Abundant Life

In John 10:10-11, Jesus says:

> *The thief comes only to steal and kill and destroy; I have come that they may have life, and have it to the full. I am the good shepherd. The good shepherd lays down His life for the sheep.*

The second part of verse 10 in the New King James Version reads, "*I have come that they may have life, and that they may have it more abundantly.*" The Lord Jesus Christ wants to give us the highest kind of life. He desires to replace our diminished and death-filled existence with one that is vital, fulfilling, rewarding, abundant, and eternal.

I truly love the Gospel of John. One of the primary reasons why the Gospel of John is so compelling is because it gives us a profound picture of the person and work of Jesus Christ. Perhaps no other book drives home more clearly the truth that Jesus Christ is the Son of God who came to give us life. John states his purpose in writing this beautiful Gospel in chapter 20, verse 31. There he writes:

> *But these* [things] *are written that you may believe that Jesus is the Christ, the Son of God, and that by believing you may have life in His name.*

In the Gospel of John, "life," "eternal life," "everlasting life," or "abundant life" is more than animated physical existence. Life is connection to God in vital relationship. Jesus says in John 17:3, "*Now this is eternal life: that they may know You, the only true God, and Jesus Christ, whom You have sent.*" He says in John 6:63

that the Holy Spirit gives life. Therefore, according to the Gospel of John, life is a personal relationship with God through His Son, Jesus Christ, by the power of the Holy Spirit. It also involves the full range of blessings that come with that personal relationship.

According to the Gospel of John, salvation is the entry point into the abundant life that Jesus describes. John 3:16 tells us that God loved the world so much *"that He gave His one and only Son, that whoever believes in Him shall not perish but have eternal life."* Verse 17 continues, *"For God did not send His Son into the world to condemn the world, but to save the world through Him."* Jesus Christ is our Lord and Savior. He cleanses us from all unrighteousness, and He gives us full access to the Heavenly Father. He fills us with the Holy Spirit. He rescues us from hell and from the things that diminish or destroy us in our spirits, minds, bodies, relationships, and other areas of our humanity.

The Lord seeks to save us in all areas of our lives. He wants to save us spiritually, mentally, emotionally, and physically. He desires to save us from sin and spiritual death, fear, addictions, mental illness, demonic entities, despair, emotional bondage, physical sickness, and ultimately physical death. Christ wants to offer wholeness to us. He wants to bring His life, health, peace, and freedom to the totality of our lives.

For some people, discussions about eternal life and abundant life cause them immediately to think about Heaven and the future. Without a doubt, Jesus Christ prepares us for a fantastic life with Him in the future. I certainly look forward to that fabulous day when, as the Book of Revelation tells us, *"There will be no more death or mourning or crying or pain, for the old order of things has passed away"* (Rev. 21:4b). That is going to be an exciting day, indeed!

However, the abundant life that God gives to us is not only for the future. In John 6:47, Jesus declares that the one who believes in Him possesses life in the present. Christ wants His people to have abundant life—to live life to the fullest—right now. He wants us to be free from the power and bondage of sin, sickness, and satan. The Lord wants us to experience the best that He has to offer while we are living here on the earth. Jesus Christ came to give us a life of abundance that begins now and continues throughout eternity.

Abundance, by any definition, involves more than what is sufficient. A basic definition of the word *abundance* is "fullness to overflowing." In the Old Testament, God reveals Himself as *El Shaddai*, which roughly means "the God of abundance" [author's translation]. In the New Testament, Paul speaks of God's ability to do *"exceedingly abundantly above"* (Eph. 3:20 NKJV) all that we could ask or think. The words *"exceedingly abundantly above"* (NIV: *"immeasurably more"*) capture the excessiveness and generosity with which God pours out His favor. God is a God of infinite liberality; His idea of blessing far exceeds what human beings can imagine.

Now, please be sober in your understanding. God is not going to fulfill every materialistic or worldly desire that we may have, but He is going to meet our needs out of His abundant resources in Jesus Christ. As Paul declares in Philippians 4:19, *"And my God will meet all your needs according to His glorious riches in Christ Jesus."* I love the words of Psalm 84:11: *"...The Lord bestows favor and honor; no good thing does He withhold from those whose walk is blameless."* Similarly, in Psalm 34:10, David declares, *"The lions may grow weak and hungry, but those who seek the Lord lack no good thing."* If we lack joy, He will give us joy. If we lack peace, He will give us peace. If we lack resources, He will give us resources. Whatever we may lack in our lives, the Lord is willing and able to provide. The Lord wants only what is best for us.

In John 10:11 Jesus says, *"I am the good shepherd."* His goodness means that He is the source of life and all its benefits. We know that the Lord is good because He does good things. The

Lord heals bodies, regulates minds, and restores relationships. He defeats darkness and changes lives. Everything the Lord does is good. The essential goodness of the Lord is one of the foundational realities on which rests our faith.

Jesus Christ is not only good, but He also is a shepherd. A shepherd is present among the sheep, living with them and providing everything that they need. In the 23rd Psalm, David speaks of the Lord personally as *"my shepherd."*[9] The Lord does not just care in general or in the abstract; He cares about us individually. Our specific concerns are very important to God. Because the Lord is a personal shepherd, David proclaims, *"I shall not be in want."* Like David, we can trust the Lord to provide for us. The Lord Jesus Christ can feed thousands of people with a few fish and loaves of bread (see Matt. 14:13-21; Mark 6:30-44; Luke 9:10-17; John 6:1-15). He can create wine for a wedding with several jars of water (see John 2:1-11). Christ can even pay taxes by withdrawing money from the mouth of a fish (see Matt. 17:24-27). The Lord is a provider, and He has countless ways to meet our needs. He cares so much for His sheep that He gave His very life for us. His supreme act of goodness and provision was His sacrificial death on the cross. We will examine more about this loving act of salvation in Chapter 3.

Twelve Daily Affirmations Based on this Chapter

I challenge you to repeat the following 12 affirmations, which I have created from the material in Chapter 1. You may wish to write down additional affirmations and recite them on a daily basis. Notice that each statement is in the first person. Some things are easier to embrace when we know that they are true in our individual lives and not just true in general. God loves the world, but He also loves you. God is good to all His creation, but He also wants to reveal His goodness to you personally. It is my hope that as you affirm the truth of this chapter and others, you will grow stronger in your faith and deeper in your relationship with the Lord.

1. God loves me. He cares for me intimately and personally.

2. God is the source of my life, health, happiness, and well-being.

3. God desires to be in a vital relationship with me.

4. I am very special to the Creator and Sustainer of the universe.

5. Salvation is available to me through the Lord Jesus Christ.

6. The Holy Spirit will cause my character and actions to conform to those of the Savior.

7. I reject the enemy and all his evil works.

8. I commit myself to God's will, authority, power, and instruction.

9. God is with me now. His presence keeps me safe and secure.

10. God is good and He is on my side, even when bad things occur in my life.

11. I look forward to Heaven, but I want the best life possible while I am on earth.

12. The Lord's vision for me is one of wholeness. My life in Christ is full and complete.

A Simple Challenge to the Reader

The Heavenly Father wants to reveal Himself to you personally. He wants you to know His ways, to feel His love, and to experience His abundant life. I would like to encourage you right now to take a moment to ask God to do something special and unique for you during the next few days. For this exercise, do not tell God how to move in your life; simply allow Him to be creative. You can offer up a short prayer such as, "Heavenly Father, I want to know You better and to do Your will. Please reveal Yourself to me in every area of my life."

Now, for the next several days as you study the Word, read this book, engage in prayer, tend to your garden, drive to your office, attend church, work at your desk, or go about your daily routine, do so with a receptive and open heart. Trust that God will indeed do something for you that you will recognize. Sometimes God is dramatic, but oftentimes He is very subtle in the way that He operates. Wait for Him with an attitude of expectation. He has good things in store for you!

> *Truly my soul silently waits for God; from Him comes my salvation* (Psalm 62:1 NKJV).

> *The Lord is good to those who wait for Him, to the soul who seeks Him* (Lamentations 3:25 NKJV).

A Prayer for Abundant Life and Well-Being

The following prayer is not meant to be a formula but a model. I hope that it will inspire you to develop your own creative, heartfelt prayers. Prayer is a great privilege that God has given to His children. The Heavenly Father waits for you to come to Him in fellowship and faith.

> *Heavenly Father, I thank You for the access that I have to You through Jesus Christ by the power of the Holy Spirit. I yield myself to the authority of the triune God. I surrender my requests to the will of the Father, the Lordship of Christ, and the direction of the Spirit.*

> *Heavenly Father, I know from Your Word that You desire life, peace, and well-being for Your children. Jesus Christ said, "The thief comes only to steal and kill and destroy; I have come that they may have life, and have it*

to the full—I have come that they may have life, and that they may have it more abundantly" (see John 10:10). *Father, I know that Your will is a life of abundance for me. Abundance, by any definition, always speaks of more than what is sufficient. In fact, Heavenly Father, You have revealed yourself as El Shaddai, the God of Abundance. Hallowed be Your name and the name of Your Son, Jesus Christ. Help me, Holy Spirit, to experience the abundant and eternal life of God, which Jesus Christ makes possible.*

Heavenly Father, You are good, so I know that I can expect good things from You. Consequently, things that steal, kill, or destroy are not from You. I reject the things that are not from You, and I embrace everything that does indeed come from You. I wholly surrender myself to You, O God, in full appreciation of the person and work of Christ. I ask You, Holy Spirit, to apply to me the benefits of the work of Christ as they relate to the following petitions. [At this time, bring your specific petitions to the Lord in prayer.] *Father, I believe that my requests are consistent with Your will. I invite You to refine them so that they more fully represent what Your desires are for my life. In the name of the Lord Jesus Christ, I pray. Amen.*

Chapter Summary

1. The triune God is the Creator and Sustainer of all things.

2. God desires for us to enjoy a close, personal relationship with Him.

3. God is reliable. He is with us even during the most difficult circumstances.

4. Christ came to provide abundant life to the children of God (see John 10:10).

5. Christ is the Good Shepherd who gave His life for the sheep (see John 10:11ff.).

Reflection/Discussion Questions

1. What new insights did you receive from reading this chapter?

2. Who is God? What is He like? What does He expect of you?

3. Do you know Jesus Christ as your personal Lord and Savior?

4. What is sin? What are the effects of sin?

5. What is salvation? From what types of things does Jesus Christ save us?

6. What does the word *reliable* mean? How does the reliability of God encourage you personally?

7. How does abundant life relate to eternal life?

8. What are some practical ways in which you can experience more fully the abundant life that Jesus Christ provides?

Practical Applications and Activities

1. On a sheet of paper or on your computer, write about several broken areas in your personal life that need healing. What hope does this chapter offer you concerning these areas?

2. Tell a family member or friend about what you learned in this chapter.

3. Set aside several minutes a day to thank God for the salvation that He extends to you through Jesus Christ.

4. Locate several Bible passages in which people received salvation as forgiveness of sins.

5. Locate several Bible passages in which people received salvation as physical healing.

6. Locate several Bible passages in which people received benefits of salvation in other ways (e.g., deliverance from evil spirits).

7. Find several opportunities to pray for people about the different challenges they are facing in life.

8. Record in a journal any major instructions that you believe God has given to you recently.

CHAPTER 2

Salvation and Wholeness in the Ministry of Jesus Christ

We are now recovering the full proclamation of the good news, that salvation is for the whole person and that Jesus came to bring us the fullness of life in every possible dimension.

If the good news is that Christ came to save us, then the power to save has to be there. If the power to save us extends to the whole person, part of the very message of salvation is that Christ came to heal us—spirit, mind, emotions, and body.

—Francis MacNutt[1]

THE MESSIAH'S MISSION OF SALVATION AND WHOLENESS IN LUKE 4:16-21

In Luke 4:16-21, the Lord Jesus Christ describes a special anointing on His life and ministry. He declares that God has anointed Him to bring salvation and wholeness to broken humanity. His message is one of good news, healing, and liberation for all humankind, especially the poor, the suffering, and the oppressed.

The anointing is a popular subject in some Christian settings today. Some equate the anointing with heightened emotion or goose bumps. Others do not think that the anointing is present in a church service unless the preacher whoops, or there is dancing in the aisles, or people fall under the power of the Holy Spirit. There certainly is nothing wrong with having energetic church services, but the anointing is not the same thing as human emotion. The anointing (literally, a smearing with oil) is the person and power of the Holy Spirit. The Holy Spirit enables God's people to do good works on earth. God empowered Jesus Christ to bring salvation and wholeness to broken humanity. This is the real purpose of the anointing.

In Luke 4:16-21, Jesus reads from Isaiah 61:1-2, a prophecy about the coming of the Messiah (or the Christ, or the Anointed One). Isaiah describes the Messiah as one who would deliver Israel from captivity. Jesus boldly claims the present and personal fulfillment of this passage in His ministry. Jesus is the Messiah to which the Old Testament points. He is the Christ whose ministry of preaching, teaching, and healing will be good news to everyone, especially the poor. In the ministry of Jesus, the era of God's salvation has now arrived!

Jesus declares that the Spirit of God has anointed Him: (1) to preach the Gospel to the poor; (2) to heal the brokenhearted; (3) to proclaim liberty to the captives and recovery of sight to the blind; (4) to set at liberty those who are oppressed; and (5) to proclaim the acceptable year of the Lord (see Luke 4:18-19 NKJV). Notice how Jesus' ministry described in this text is for the whole person. Christ cares about an individual's spiritual condition, emotional state, physical health, and socioeconomic status. Each area of human experience can receive a liberating touch from Him.

Jesus says that the Spirit is upon Him to preach the Gospel or "good news." The good news is that, through Jesus Christ, we can have eternal life and enjoy an intimate relationship with God. Jesus Christ dealt with human separation from God by taking upon Himself the penalty of sin. Christ died on the cross and rose from the dead. He conquered sin and death through the cross and the resurrection. Now, human fellowship with God is possible in Christ. Eternal life and personal wholeness are now fully available to us.

Paul summarizes the way to salvation in Romans 10:9:

That if you confess with your mouth, "Jesus is Lord," and believe in your heart that God raised Him from the dead, you will be saved.

Similarly, in Acts 16:31, he states, *"Believe in the Lord Jesus, and you will be saved."* He declares in First Thessalonians 5:9, *"For God did not appoint us to suffer wrath but to receive salvation through our Lord Jesus Christ."* Christ rescues us from the terrible bondage of sin. He frees us from the hostility that has arrested our thinking and expressed itself in our actions. When we surrender ourselves to His Lordship, we experience true freedom.

When we proclaim, "Jesus Christ is Lord," we affirm that Christ is the Master and Supreme Ruler of the universe. He has all authority and all power, both in Heaven and on earth. When we accept the Lordship of Jesus Christ over our lives, we place everything that we are and everything that we own at His disposal. We commit ourselves to love Him, to obey Him, and to serve Him faithfully. Acceptance of the Lordship of Jesus Christ is the secret to true happiness and fulfillment. It is the first step to personal wholeness.

Jesus continues that God has sent Him to heal the brokenhearted and to proclaim liberty to the captives. The Lord has the power to comfort us in any situation and rescue us from any spiritual, emotional, or physical stronghold. Some of the fiercest battles that we fight occur in our minds. The enemy is a master of deception. He loves to assault our minds and emotions with fear, worry, temptations, lies, and other types of bondage. He seeks to deceive us about God, ourselves, and other people. So how do we protect our minds from the attacks of satan? I believe that the answer is threefold.

First, we must spend time with God in prayer and commit ourselves to obedience. When we walk closely with God, we will develop trust in Him, knowing that His plans for us are good. God loved us so much that He gave us the greatest gift in the universe, Jesus Christ His Son, and since God gave us Christ, He also will give us everything else that we need (see Rom. 8:32).

Second, to protect our minds from the enemy, we need to renew them through the Word of God. This is the message of Romans 12:2. The reading and especially the hearing of the Word build faith in our hearts. I encourage you to spend time each day reading, reciting, and memorizing the Bible. After a while, the Word will become a part of you and transform your thinking. As Philippians 4:8 exhorts us:

> *Whatever is true, whatever is noble, whatever is right, whatever is pure, whatever is lovely, whatever is admirable—if anything is excellent or praiseworthy—think about such things.*

Third, we need aggressively to resist ungodly thoughts. As Second Corinthians 10:5 states:

> *We demolish arguments and every pretension that sets itself up against the knowledge of God, and we take captive every thought to make it obedient to Christ.*

Sometimes we have to say to our minds, "You will be subject to Jesus Christ!" The Lord has given us the authority or right to do the will of God, and it is God's will for us to think healthy thoughts. Jesus tells us in John 8:32 that knowledge of the truth will lead to our freedom from bondage. Each day, we should ponder, repeat, and embrace the things that we know to be true.

- We know that God is good. Do not ever forget this truth!

- We know that Jesus Christ desires for us to be whole. This is His stated mission!

- We know that God is with and for us. Celebrate these realities!

- We know that God loves us. No human parent can match God's tender concern for us!

- We know that God will never leave nor forsake us. He is with you now!

- We know that Christ has already defeated the enemy. The devil's days are numbered!

- We know that Christ conquered death at Calvary. Death is now only a temporary foe!

We must allow God's truth to bring spiritual and emotional freedom to our minds.

The anointing of the Holy Spirit also can bring physical healing. Jesus includes healing and miracles as a part of His mission of salvation. In particular, He mentions the *"recovery of sight for the blind"* (Luke 4:18). Throughout His ministry, Jesus preaches the Gospel, casts out demons, heals the sick, and raises the dead. All of these are saving actions.

Jesus' healing miracles not only confirm that His teachings about salvation are true; His healing miracles also represent salvation actually taking place.[2] In fact, one of the main Greek words translated *salvation* in the New Testament also means "healing."[3] For example, in Mark's Gospel, the woman with the issue of blood says to herself, *"If only I may touch His clothes, I shall be made well"* (Mark 5:28 NKJV). The phrase *"made well"* can be translated "saved." Jesus responds to the woman, *"Daughter, your faith has made you well. Go in peace, and be healed of your affliction"* (Mark 5:34 NKJV). I translate this verse from the Greek as follows, *"Daughter, your faith has saved you and made you whole. Walk in the healing and well-being of your salvation."* So healing is salvation occurring in the physical realm.

In the Gospels, the faith that saves is the faith that heals, and the faith that heals is the faith that saves.[4] Salvation, then, is not only the forgiveness of sin but also the availability of God's power to heal the body from sickness and disease. When Jesus Christ died on the cross, He paid the price for our sins. However, He also paid the price for the effects of sin. Sickness entered the earth because of sin. When God heals a person, He demonstrates the victory of the Lord Jesus Christ over sickness.

> *He was wounded for our transgressions, He was bruised for our iniquities; the chastisement for our peace was upon Him, and by His stripes we are healed* [healing has come to us] (Isaiah 53:5 NKJV).

The Lord is a healer! He is a healer, and no sickness can withstand His power! Jeremiah prayed: *"Heal me, O Lord, and I will be healed; save me and I will be saved, for You are the one I praise"* (Jer. 17:14).

The psalmist cried, *"O Lord my God, I called to You for help and You healed me"* (Ps. 30:2). The Lord can heal us directly or indirectly. He can heal us instantly or progressively. He can heal us supernaturally or through a doctor. He can heal us in a church service or in a hospital room. In numerous places and in countless ways, the Great Physician is at work. The Lord can cure cancer, diabetes, AIDS, kidney failure, arthritis, blood conditions, multiple sclerosis, heart and liver problems, skin diseases, nerve damage, high blood pressure, mental disorders, lupus, drug addiction, demonic attacks, and any other issues that we face.

I can vividly remember the healing of a thyroid condition around 15 years ago. The evangelist Oral Roberts, who was visiting the church I attended, prayed for a dear woman who had a very large and very visible goiter. Within a few seconds of the prayer, the goiter decreased in size before our very eyes. The healing power of the Lord Jesus Christ was evident to all.

In Luke 4:16-21, it is clear that God anointed Jesus Christ to preach the Gospel while He was on earth. Now, the Lord has commissioned the Church to continue His ministry. We now have the right and the charge to proclaim the fullness of God's salvation in Christ. When we face satanic and demonic opposition, we can say, "In the name of Jesus Christ, I command you to leave my presence." When we face unholy thoughts, we can say, "Mind, you will be subject to the Lordship of Christ." When we face crippling fear, we can say, *"God has not given* [me] *a spirit of fear, but of power and of love and of a sound mind"* (2 Tim. 1:7 NKJV). When we face sickness and disease, we can say, "My body must come into alignment with the perfect will of God. Lord, I receive the physical healing that You extend to me right now." When we face anything internal or external that opposes God's will, we can say, "Mountain of opposition, be removed and cast into the sea" (see Matt. 21:21).

The Lord Jesus Christ wants to make us whole. He wants to save us in every area of our lives. He wants to forgive our sins, to free us from the bondage of fear, to rescue us from the snare of the evil one, and to bring physical healing to our bodies. In the name of Jesus Christ, receive God's wholeness today!

A Ministry of Compassion: Jesus Reveals the Heart of God

The heart of God is full of compassion for broken humanity. Compassion is "love in action." It is the ability to feel what someone else feels, and it involves not only an awareness of the pain of another but also an inward desire to relieve the pain. The Old Testament reveals compassion as an essential aspect of God's nature (e.g., see Exod. 34:6-7; Ps. 86:15; 145:8-9; Lam. 3:22-23). The New Testament also witnesses to the compassion of God, particularly in the ministry of Jesus Christ (e.g., see Matt. 9:35-36; 14:14; Mark 1:40-42; 8:2-3; Luke 7:11-17).

The Bible teaches us that God came to earth as a human being, in the person of Jesus Christ. God's identification with humanity is called the Incarnation. The miracle of the Incarnation demonstrates that God does not just pity us from afar. He actually shares in our human experiences: our joys and sorrows, our successes and failures, our triumphs and tragedies. Jesus can relate to us because He walked in our shoes (see Heb. 4:14-16).

When God came to earth in the person of Jesus Christ, He most clearly demonstrated His deep compassion for us. Indeed, the whole life and ministry of the Savior reveal His compassion. Through His teachings, through His healings, through His miracles, and through His suffering and death on the cross, Christ reveals to us that God is on our side; He feels our pain; and He wants to rescue us from the things that diminish or destroy us in our spirits, minds, bodies, relationships, and other areas of our humanity. Charles Wesley proclaimed:

> Jesus, thou art all compassion,
> Pure unbounded love thou art;
> Visit us with thy salvation;
> Enter every trembling heart.[5]

One of my favorite accounts of the Lord's compassion is Luke 7:11-17. In the passage, Jesus Christ encounters a dear woman. The woman is a widow, so she has lost her husband. The joyful companionship that he once provided is no more. Some of you reading this book may have experienced the death of a spouse or other loved one. You can relate to the tremendous grief that the woman must have felt. Now she has lost her only son and her only remaining means of financial support. Life is so unfair at times! One can only imagine what the woman's prayer time may have sounded like: "Dear God, what is going on? Not my boy; he is all that I had left! He was in the prime of his life; now he is gone! Why did this have to happen to me?"

The poor woman in our story is heartbroken. She is a mother who is distressed over the loss of a child. She is a woman who will never experience the joy of having grandchildren. She is alone, emotionally vulnerable, and probably weeping uncontrollably; however, her anguish does not escape the watchful eyes of the Savior.

When Jesus sees the woman, her pain resonates with Him. Luke 7:13 states, *"When the Lord saw her, He had compassion on her"* (NKJV). The Greek word translated *compassion* in this text literally means "a stirring in the intestines" or "a movement in the inward parts." We might say that Jesus' heart went out to the widow. With great love and care in His voice, Jesus Christ says to the grieving woman, *"Do not weep"* (Luke 7:13 NKJV)! What a strange thing to say at a funeral! What the Lord asks of the widow may seem impossible; however, Jesus always challenges us to take a step of faith. In the presence of the living Christ, God strengthens our faith and transforms our deepest sorrows.

Compassion always leads to action. Luke 7:14-15 says:

Then [Christ] *came and touched the open coffin, and those who carried him stood still. And He said, "Young man,*

I say to you, arise." [The dead man] *sat up and began to speak. And* [Christ] *presented him to his mother* (NKJV).

What an impressive demonstration of love, power, and compassion! Jesus takes a situation of tremendous grief and sadness and turns it into an occasion of immense joy and worship.

Verse 16 describes the reaction of the amazed crowd. The people declare that Jesus is a great prophet and that God has visited His people. The people probably are comparing Jesus to the two Old Testament prophets, Elijah and Elisha, both who prayed to raise dead sons back to life; however, Jesus is a prophet far greater than Elijah or Elisha. Jesus Christ is God in the flesh. He is the resurrection and the life in human form. In the person of Jesus Christ, God truly has visited His people in a powerful way.

In verse 17, Luke concludes the miracle account by noting the spread of Jesus' fame throughout Judea and the surrounding region. Now, 2,000 years later, Jesus' fame has not diminished. He is still changing lives today and bringing comfort to those in need.

There are many people reading this book who need a fresh encounter with the compassion of Jesus Christ. Maybe life has dealt a major blow like the woman in our text. Sicknesses, deaths of loved ones, natural disasters, tragedies, and other negative realities can enter into our worlds at any time, often without warning. We definitely need God's strength and direction when facing situations that are beyond our control.

Yet, there are often bad decisions that we make that lead to difficult circumstances in our lives. Perhaps you are reaping the consequences of a poor decision. There have been many unwise decisions I have made throughout my life, and I just needed God to cover me. I could not provide any excuses. I could not blame God, my circumstances, other people, or even the devil. I was completely to blame, and I just had to cry out, "Lord, I need Your help!" The Lord has never failed to help me during the low points of my life. In fact, He has always worked out those difficult times for my greatest good.

The compassion of Christ is available to all of us, and I pray that you will come to experience His awesome compassion for yourself. All will agree that Christ is compassionate, in general; however, I want you to be able to say with conviction, "Christ is compassionate to me!" Hebrews 13:8 declares, *"Jesus Christ is the same yesterday and today and forever."* Therefore, He is still being moved with compassion today and changing the lives of the hurting.

The compassion of Jesus Christ reveals that He truly is the Savior. He came to make us whole in every way. He came to rescue us from the things that diminish or destroy us in our spirits, minds, bodies, relationships, and other aspects of our humanity. There is no aspect of human experience that is beyond His saving power. As the widow in our text learned, not even physical death is a barrier for our Lord. Nothing is too difficult for the Lord to accomplish!

Forsaking All, I Touch Him—Appropriating the Benefits of Salvation by Faith

Mark 5:25-34 recounts the story of the woman with the issue (flow) of blood. In reaching for the hem of Jesus' garment, the woman touched Christ with her faith and received the miracle that she needed from Him. Her faith enabled her to receive wholeness from the Savior. Notice that the first letter of each of the first five words in the title of this section form the word *faith*.

Probably many readers of this book are praying for miracles. Perhaps you have tried everything that you know to do in the natural, but it seems like nothing is working. You are still losing life, health, resources, and strength. There is good news for you, though:

God has given you the privilege of touching the Savior! The same miracle-working Lord in the Bible is available to you today. No matter what your problem may be, the solution is in Jesus Christ.

In our text, Mark introduces us to a woman. We do not know her name or family history. The only thing that we know about the woman is that she has a great need. She has had a flow of blood for 12 long years. Some scholars suggest that her condition is a hemorrhage from the womb, maybe cancer of the uterus, but from Mark's description, it is impossible for us to know for sure. All we know is that the woman is a victim of persistent bleeding.

Yet, the issue of blood is not the only problem confronting the woman. According to the Jewish law, she is ritually unclean and socially unacceptable. Leviticus forbids her to touch others or to receive a touch from them (see Lev. 15:19). In addition to her issue of blood, the woman more than likely suffers from depression, isolation, and embarrassment.

Moreover, the woman's physicians are all useless. As I researched some of the ancient treatments for a hemorrhaging woman, I discovered a number of very strange remedies indeed.[6] One remedy consisted of drinking wine mixed with powdered rubber, a certain type of salt, and various plants. Another remedy consisted of a dose of Persian onions boiled in wine administered with the command, "Arise out of your flow of blood!" A third treatment involved carrying the ashes of an ostrich egg in a linen or cotton rag. Talk about your bad HMO plans! Some physicians even prescribed sudden shock or other folk remedies. Of course, these treatments have not helped the poor woman in our text. Mark 5:26 indicates that the woman has suffered many things from many physicians. She has spent all her money, but instead of getting better, she has grown quite worse.

The hemorrhaging woman, like so many of us, has a problem. She has an issue (flow) of blood and many other life issues (problems), yet no one has provided any answers for her: not her doctors, not her family, not her friends, not the rabbis—no one has been able to help this poor woman. Now she has exhausted all her natural options. She is sick, tired, and weak—and the awful smell of blood is certainly overwhelming at this point! She is broke, hurting, alone, and in great distress.

The situation looks bleak for her, and perhaps the woman is tempted to throw in the towel after so many years of suffering, but she hears the good news that the Savior has arrived on the scene. There is no aspect of human experience that is beyond the saving power of Jesus Christ. Personal sin, physical infirmities, mental illnesses, emotional bondages, demonic entities, natural disasters, and other destructive realities ultimately find their defeat with the Lord Jesus Christ. Salvation is rescue from the things that diminish or destroy us in our spirits, minds, bodies, relationships, and other areas of our humanity.

Some of the freedom that God offers to us in Christ awaits us in the future. Until that time, we still contend with sickness, poverty, persecution, and physical death. God has ordained a future day in which He will *"wipe away every tear from* [our] *eyes;* [a day when] *there shall be no more death, no sorrow, nor crying... no more pain..."* (Rev. 21:4 NKJV).

Therefore, God is operating on a timetable. Yet, even though God is working on a timetable, we can rejoice right now because anything that we need and anything that we will ever need are already present in the person of Jesus Christ.

If we have Christ in our lives, we can face tsunamis, hurricanes, earthquakes, fires, sicknesses, financial troubles, tragedies, hardships, and suffering with the assurance that God's presence and power will sustain us. God has never promised to prevent trials from coming into our lives, but He has promised to be with us in our trials (e.g., see Ps. 23:4; Isa. 41:10; 43:2). Because of the Lord's faithfulness, we can completely put our trust in Him.

Even if you have been waiting for many years for your breakthrough, do not lose heart. God still loves you, and He is still with you. It took 12 years for the woman with the issue of blood to get her miracle, but her divine appointment finally came. So keep trusting God and He will manifest Himself to you at just the right moment. Your miracle may even be today!

The woman with the issue of blood experienced the saving power of Christ in the form of physical healing, and I pray that you also will experience the power of the Son of God in the manner that you need most in your life. Have faith. The story of the woman with the issue of blood teaches us a lot about the dynamics of faith. Faith is unwavering trust in God that causes us to believe God's Word and to act on it. Faith requires a commitment to God and the Lord Jesus Christ from every part of us: our minds, wills, emotions, and bodies. The cry of faith is, "Lord, I put my full trust in You! I yield myself to You! I surrender my life to You! I look to You as the fulfillment of every need that I have!" Even during the periods when God seems silent, faith will cause us to follow Him in trust (e.g., see Isa. 50:10).

I would like to address three key aspects of faith that our text reveals. First, the woman with the issue of blood heard about Jesus (verse 27). Hearing and faith are inseparable partners. Paul tells us in Romans 10:17, *"So then faith comes by hearing, and hearing by the word of God"* (NKJV). The woman with the issue of blood developed faith in Jesus Christ after hearing the many reports of His mighty exploits. She probably said to herself:

This man has authority to cast out demons! He has power to heal all types of diseases! He can cure leprosy with a word and reverse the effects of paralysis! He can calm a raging storm and can even raise the dead! This man has power over nature, power over satan, power over sickness, and power over death itself! Nothing is impossible with Him!

The woman with the issue of blood heard about Jesus. She heard that Jesus saves, heals, delivers, and sets captives free. The things that the woman heard strengthened her faith, encouraged her, and convinced her of the tremendous power of the Lord Jesus Christ.

Have you heard anything wonderful about Jesus? Perhaps you have heard that He is a Way-maker, a Heart-fixer, and a Power-giver. The more good things that we hear about the Lord, the stronger our faith will become. When we hear the preaching of the Gospel, we develop trust and confidence that God is willing and able to save us, bless us, and meet our needs. The woman with the issue of blood heard about Christ and became convinced of His awesome power.

The woman with the issue of blood not only heard with her natural ears, she also heard with her "spiritual ears." There was a revelation in her spirit that God would heal her. Even if we happen to be deaf or hard of hearing in the natural, we can still hear the Lord speak to our spirits. Sometimes the outward signs may point to defeat and disappointment. Sometimes the doctors have done all they can do. Sometimes it appears there is no hope left. Yet, we must never forget that God has the final word. Whenever we face difficult problems, we must discover what God says about the situation.

There are many strange and conflicting voices in the world, but we must filter out the things that do not line up with God's

Word. The Medieval Catholic monk Thomas à Kempis wrote, "Blessed are the ears that catch the accents of divine whispering, and pay no heed to the murmurings of the world."[7] Sometimes the voice of human opinion will try to gain entry into our lives. We must shut it out. Sometimes the voice of past failure will try to discourage us from believing God for a miracle. We must shut it out. Sometimes the voice of doubt and skepticism will attempt to quench our faith. We must shut it out. Sometimes the voice of the enemy will try to drown out the voice of the Lord. We must shut it out. When we develop ears that are sensitive to the voice of the Lord, our faith will grow. Faith comes through hearing the Word of God.

Faith was built within the woman's heart after she heard about Christ. Then the faith that was built in her heart caused the woman to act. This is the second great lesson that the passage teaches us: faith requires action. A faith action is simply a positive response to what we hear. The woman with the issue of blood was convinced that Jesus Christ was the solution to her problem, so she pursued Him with intensity and resolve.

Faith will cause you to push through a crowd to get to the Master. Faith will cause you to forget about your limitations and call out to the Savior. Faith will cause you to come into the presence of God to ask for mercy. The woman with the issue of blood acted on her faith. She kept saying to herself, *"If only I may touch His clothes, I shall be made well"* (Mark 5:28 NKJV). Sometimes we must prophesy to ourselves and encourage ourselves in the Lord. Sometimes we must remind ourselves that God is love, that God is good, and that God is faithful. Sometimes we must act on what we know to be true, even when no one else seems to understand what we are going through.

The woman with the issue of blood acted on the things she heard about the love and power of God in Jesus Christ. I can imagine the excitement that must have flooded through the very core of her being.

> Finally, after twelve long years, this is my big chance! Surely, Jesus will save me from this infirmity. Surely, Jesus will heal my body and make me well. Those doctors that I visited were all useless. The only thing that they have relieved me of is my money! The priests have told me that I am unclean! No one has wanted to be near me! Jesus is my only hope! Jesus is my only option! Jesus is my only recourse! Jesus is my source of wholeness! I must get to Jesus! I must get to the Savior! I must get to the Master! I must meet this man from Galilee, and when I touch Him, He will set me free!

This dear woman came to a point of expectancy. She came to a point of belief in the "nowness" of God. She knew that the name "Jesus" means, "Yahweh is Salvation Now." Whatever she needed was present in Jesus Christ. Although she had waited for over a decade, she knew by divine revelation that now was her appointed time of blessing, favor, and freedom. Now was the time for her to take a risk of faith. She probably said with determination:

> I am not going to let the crowd stop me. I am not going to let past disappointments stop me. I am not going to let the Jewish law stop me. I am going to receive a miracle today! I am going to receive all that God has for me today!

We all need to have the same type of attitude displayed by the woman with the issue of blood. If we truly believe something, then our actions will conform to that belief. Our actions typically need not be complicated ones. Usually, God only requires us to take simple steps of faith. Yet, extraordinary power can be released in our lives when we act on the things that we truly believe.

If we believe that God will do what He has promised, then we will cling to His promises with confidence, assurance, and anticipation. Even if the miracle takes a while, we will stand on the truth that God always knows what is best for us. If we truly believe something, then our actions will conform to that belief.

Faith requires hearing and action. The third lesson from this story is that the goal of faith is to touch Jesus. Matthew and Luke declare that the woman with the issue of blood touched the hem or border of Jesus' garment. What the woman was in fact doing was reaching for the tassels attached to the corners of Jesus' prayer shawl. The corners of these prayer shawls often were called "wings." The woman probably was familiar with the words of Malachi 4:2. The prophet Malachi predicted that when the Sun of Righteousness (or the Messiah) would arise, He would have *"healing in His wings"* (NKJV). The woman probably remembered the prophecy and thought to herself, "If I am going to receive a healing today, then the healing is going to be found in the wings of the Messiah." By faith, she acted on her belief, touched the hem of Jesus' garment, and received a miracle.

The woman with the issue of blood physically touched Jesus' garment. However, Jesus felt a tug not just on His garment but on His heart as well. There was nothing magical or extraordinary about His clothing. The real point of this story is that the woman put her trust in the Lord Jesus Christ. By her actions, the woman was saying:

> Jesus, I am reaching out by faith to declare that You are the Messiah! I am reaching out to declare Your supreme Lordship! I am reaching out to acknowledge Your healing authority! I am reaching out to touch Your heart!

The woman trusted Jesus so strongly that He could feel the pull. Verse 30 states that Jesus knew within Himself that power had gone out of Him. The most radical kind of faith focuses so intently on Jesus Christ that the problem pales in comparison to His majesty. In the words of the songwriter:

Turn your eyes upon Jesus,
Look full in His wonderful face,
And the things of earth will grow strangely dim
In the light of His glory and grace.[8]

The Lord Jesus Christ is the object of our faith. God wants to give us more than the things for which we ask; He wants to give us a relationship with Himself through faith in His Son, Jesus Christ. Genuine faith has the Lord Jesus Christ as the object of that faith. Of course, we want to be healed! Of course, we want to be blessed! Of course, we want to escape the problems that we are facing! Yet, we must get to the point where Jesus Christ is more important to us than the things after which we seek.

The woman with the issue of blood pursued Christ and received much more than just physical healing; she also received wholeness. Jesus said, *"Daughter, your faith has made you well. Go in peace"* (Mark 5:34 NKJV). As I mentioned above, I translate the verse as follows: *"Daughter, your faith has saved you and made you whole. Walk in the healing and well-being of your salvation."* The woman touched Jesus with her faith, and Christ touched her with His power. His saving power brought her into God's Kingdom, dried up her infirmity, and radically changed her life.

What I like about the woman with the issue of blood is that she pursued Christ with reckless abandon. She touched Jesus with her faith and received the victory that she needed. Like this courageous woman of faith, if we will pursue the Lord with all our hearts, we too can receive the wholeness we need from Him.

We began this chapter with a discussion of the anointing of the Holy Spirit. My prayer for you is that the Lord will empower you with His Spirit to meet each of life's challenges and to accomplish each task that the Heavenly Father wills for you to accomplish. Put your trust in the Lord, and do not allow your circumstances to weaken your faith. God is greater than your circumstances! Any brokenness that presently exists in your life can be healed today as you allow the Savior to minister to your needs. In the words of the late John Wimber:

> O let the Son of God enfold you with His Spirit
> and His love.
> Let Him fill your heart and satisfy your soul.
> O let Him have those things that hold you and
> His Spirit like a dove
> Will descend upon your life and make you whole.[9]

A PRAYER FOR SALVATION AND WHOLENESS
FOR THE TOTAL PERSON

Preliminary Issues:

As you prepare to pray for wholeness, I suggest that you repent of any known sins in your life. Ask God for the strength to release the emotional poison of resentment, bitterness, and unforgiveness. Forgive those who have harmed you in the past and forgive yourself for the mistakes that you have made. Also, release any grudges that you may be holding against God. No matter what you are facing: (1) God loves you; (2) God is with you; (3) God will continue to sustain you; and (4) God will work out your situation for your greatest good. Trust Him today!

Actual Prayer (Adapt as the Holy Spirit Leads):

Heavenly Father, I humble myself in worship before You, and I cry out to You with all my heart. I look beyond my problems, and I declare my love for You. You, Dear

God, are worthy of glory, honor, and praise. You are infinite in grace, rich in mercy, and liberal in compassion. I reverence and respect all that You are, and I am grateful for everything You have done. I thank You most of all for the gift of Your Son, Jesus Christ, my Lord. It is because of Christ that I receive salvation and wholeness. It is because of Him that I have access to You, Heavenly Father. It is because of the Lord that I obtain freedom from the power and the bondage of sin and satan.

Heavenly Father, I believe that it is Your will not only to bring healing to my body, but also to bring renewal to my spirit, peace to my mind, and wholeness to every aspect of my life. Therefore, I petition You to extend Your mighty hand of grace to me. I seek wholeness in every sense of the term. I desire Your salvation, healing, blessing, renewal, restoration, abiding presence, transformation, deliverance, prosperity, peace, guidance, help, strength, and favor.

Father, I pray that You will frustrate the plans of the enemy, destroy his evil works, and rescue me from the things that diminish or destroy me in my spirit, mind, body, relationships, and other areas of my humanity. I stand against every source of pain, affliction, and worry in my life in the name of the Lord Jesus Christ. I stand against fear and spiritual opposition of every kind. I also stand against every sickness and disease.

By faith, I command my body, mind, and spirit to receive the wholeness that You extend to me right now. Come into alignment with the perfect will of God. Be made whole in Jesus' name. Be restored in Jesus' name. I invite the divine order of God into every situation in my life. Finally, Heavenly Father, I give You glory, honor, and praise. Thank You for hearing my prayers. In the name of the Lord Jesus Christ, I pray. Amen.

Chapter Summary

1. The mission of Jesus Christ is one of salvation and wholeness for broken humanity.

2. Jesus Christ saves us from sin and its effects.

3. Jesus Christ forgives sins, regulates minds, heals bodies, mends relationships, and rescues us from the things that diminish or destroy us in all areas of our lives.

4. The ministry of Jesus Christ reveals the love and compassion of God.

5. We appropriate the benefits of salvation through faith.

6. The story of the woman with the issue (flow) of blood teaches us several fundamental principles of faith: 1) faith requires hearing; 2) faith requires action; and 3) faith requires us to touch Jesus (i.e., pursue Him with intensity).

REFLECTION/DISCUSSION QUESTIONS

1. What new insights did you receive from reading this chapter?

2. In your own words, what is the mission of Jesus Christ in Luke 4:16-21?

3. What is salvation? What is healing? How are salvation and healing related?

4. What does the word *compassion* mean?

5. What is faith? How is faith involved in achieving personal wholeness?

6. Do you need a breakthrough in your life? How does the story of the widow from Nain encourage you? How does the story of the woman with the issue of blood encourage you?

Practical Applications and Activities

1. Find several Bible verses that contain the word *Gospel* and memorize them.

2. Tell a family member or friend about what you learned in this chapter.

3. Pray with someone for physical healing, and record the results in a journal.

4. Write your own personal prayer for wholeness.

CHAPTER 3

The Cross and Personal Transformation

On a hill far away, stood an old rugged cross,
The emblem of suffering and shame;
And I love that old cross where the dearest and best
For a world of lost sinners was slain.

In the old rugged cross, stained with blood so divine,
A wondrous beauty I see;
For 'twas on that old cross Jesus suffered and died,
To pardon and sanctify me.[1]

THE CENTRALITY OF THE CROSS

According to the apostle Paul, the central theme of preaching must be *"Jesus Christ and Him crucified"* (1 Cor. 2:1-2). Paul also declares in Galatians 2:20 that he has been crucified with Christ, indicating his identification with the work of the Savior. To be crucified literally means "to die on a cross." Paul appreciated the benefits that came from Christ's death on the cross, and just like Paul, we also profit from the Lord's painful ordeal. Jesus Christ and His work on the cross are the foundation upon which the Christian faith is built. The good news of the Gospel is that Jesus Christ died for our sins on the cross; He was buried; He rose from the dead; and He now offers eternal life to us. The cross, then, is an essential symbol of God's salvation of humankind. The cross is a graphic reminder of the terrible price Jesus paid to secure our salvation. If we are to experience personal transformation and wholeness in our lives, then we must accept Jesus Christ as Lord and Savior and embrace the message of the cross.

If you saw the movie *The Passion of the Christ* or read the Gospel accounts of the Savior's agony, then you know a little something about the brutal nature of crucifixion.[2] Crucifixion was a violent, humiliating, and prolonged form of execution. Victims were savagely beaten, stripped naked, and then secured in a manner on a cross that intensified their suffering and prevented them from dying quickly. Sometimes people would hang on a cross for days and would be subject to hunger, disease, shock, or exhaustion. Death usually occurred after a slow and painful process of asphyxiation. Bodies of the crucified often were left unburied to be eaten by wild animals. The tortuous practice of crucifixion has given us the English word *excruciating,* which literally means "out of the cross."

Crucifixion was usually reserved for criminals at the lowest levels of society. The Romans typically did not crucify their citizens, only slaves or foreigners. The Jews viewed crucifixion as particularly opprobrious. Deuteronomy 21:23 states, for example: *"he who is hanged is accursed of God"* (NKJV). Paul reiterates this idea in Galatians 3:13 where he declares:

> *Christ has redeemed us from the curse of the law, having become a curse for us (for it is written, "Cursed is everyone who hangs on a tree")* (NKJV).

Both the Old and New Testaments point to the degradation experienced by the Lord Jesus Christ. Isaiah 53:3 prophesies that He would be *"despised and rejected."* Mark 15:32 states that even the criminals who were crucified with Christ ridiculed and insulted Him.

The idea of a crucified Messiah was utter foolishness to many Jews and Gentiles; yet God chose the foolishness of the cross to bring salvation to humankind (see 1 Cor. 1:18-31). On that old rugged cross, Jesus Christ died for our sins. He was savagely beaten and hung naked on that awful execution post to save the world from eternal separation from God. Christ experienced the shame of the cross so that you and I could be reconciled to God. He died in our place so that we could enjoy an everlasting relationship with God. The message of the cross is the supreme message of God's love for sinful humanity (see John 3:16-17).

The death of Jesus Christ on the cross looked like a major defeat, but actually, it led to the greatest victory in human history. The Lord endured the shame of the cross. He rose from the grave and purchased our salvation. He conquered sin, sickness, satan, and death itself. Now He is alive forevermore! The trial that you are facing will not destroy you because Jesus is alive! The personal struggle you are fighting will not defeat you because Jesus is alive! Your physical and emotional health can improve dramatically because Jesus is alive! The economic crisis in your family can be reversed because Jesus is alive! Let every problem hear the message that Jesus is alive! Let every sickness hear the message that Jesus is alive! Let fear and depression hear the message that Jesus is alive. Let every dark force tremble in fear because the Lord Jesus is alive and well.

BENEFITS OF THE CROSS

The death of Jesus Christ on the cross has given us many wonderful benefits. Let me share with you a few of these. First, the death of Jesus Christ on the cross deals with both sin and its consequences. When Jesus died on the cross, He removed the death sentence that was on our lives (see Rom. 6:23). He rescued us from the penalty of sin, so that we are now free from the power of sin. However, it gets better! One day, we shall be free from the very presence of sin and will live for all eternity without pain, violence, sickness, disease, decay, deterioration, or physical death. Because of the defeat of sin at the cross, Paul can say that Christians are now dead to sin (see Rom. 6:11). Paul's statement means that we have the power to live for God on a daily basis. The apostle Peter, in First Peter 2:24, states that Jesus *"bore our sins in His own body on the tree, that we, having died to sins, might live for righteousness"* (NKJV).

Second, the death of Jesus Christ on the cross justifies us and delivers us from the wrath of God. God is holy and just. Because God is holy, He hates sin with a passion. Because God is just, He must judge sin whenever it rears its ugly head. The consequence of God's holiness and justice for humankind is that our sins caused us to become objects of God's wrath (see Eph. 2:1-3). Because of the cross, we now escape the wrath of God. In Romans 5:9, Paul writes, *"Having now been justified by His blood, we shall be saved from wrath through Him"* (NKJV). When God justifies us, He declares us righteous. His righteousness becomes our own. When Jesus died on the cross, He endured the wrath of God and received the penalty of death that we rightfully deserved. The result is that we now stand before God free from guilt.

Third, through the death of Jesus Christ on the cross, God redeems and forgives us. According to Colossians 1:14, we *"have redemption through His blood, the forgiveness of sins"* (NKJV). Similarly, Ephesians 1:7 states, *"In Him we have redemption through His blood, the forgiveness of sins, according to the riches of His grace"* (NKJV). The word *redemption* in the text implies the payment of a ransom in order to free slaves or prisoners. We were slaves and prisoners to sin and subject to the cruel effects of sin until Jesus Christ redeemed us. Redemption means that Jesus paid a heavy price to save us. He gave His very life to purchase our salvation! To *forgive* is to free someone from what binds him or her. The word literally means "send away." When God forgives us, He frees us from bondage and sends our sins away through the precious blood of Jesus Christ.

Fourth, the death of Jesus Christ on the cross breaks the power of the enemy. Colossians 2:14-15 states that Christ disarmed, humiliated, and stripped the evil forces opposing Him and us. Although these forces are still causing trouble in the world, they will never win an ultimate victory over God's people, and their day of destruction is coming. Hebrews 2:14-15 says that through His death, Christ destroyed the devil and released us from the bondage of fear. When Jesus Christ died on the cross and rose from the dead, it was a fatal blow to satan and the kingdom of darkness. The devil no longer has any legal claim to humanity. Furthermore, the cross rendered powerless his two great weapons of sin and death. It is only a matter of time before satan and his demons face eternal torment in the lake of fire (hell).

Fifth, the death of Jesus Christ on the cross can bring physical healing. According to Isaiah 53:4 and Matthew 8:17, Jesus took up our infirmities and carried our diseases. He died on the cross to free us from the full effects of sin, which include physical sickness. Isaiah 53:5 states, *"By His stripes we are healed"* (NKJV), or "by His stripes, healing has come to us." Jesus' death on the cross makes it possible for us to receive a physical touch from God.

Some have experienced physical healing during the celebration of Holy Communion. I myself was healed of high blood sugar on a Communion Sunday (see Chapter 6). The communion elements represent the broken body and shed blood of the Savior. In First Corinthians 11:30, the apostle Paul connects the celebration with physical health. Some who had partaken of the Lord's Supper in an unworthy manner grew ill or even died prematurely.[3] Inversely, the reverential celebration of Holy Communion and the full embrace of the Lord's sacrificial work can lead to forgiveness and healing. I encourage you the next time you partake of Holy Communion to reflect on the salvation and wholeness that Jesus Christ makes possible. If you are sick, ask God to heal you as a testament to His love and power, which are seen so clearly in the sacrifice of His Son. The communion elements have no curative properties in and of themselves; however, they are a vivid reminder of the Lord's healing grace.

A sixth benefit that comes from the death of Jesus Christ on the cross is our deliverance from the finality of physical death. We will live for all eternity with the Lord. Second Timothy 1:10 says that Jesus Christ *"has abolished death and brought life and immortality to light through the gospel"* (NKJV). Hebrews 2:9 says that Jesus tasted death for everyone. Christians need not fear death because eternal life is ours through the Lord Jesus Christ.

A seventh benefit of the cross is reconciliation. To reconcile means to restore fellowship after estrangement. God created the human race to enjoy constant fellowship with Him. In the beginning, Adam and Eve enjoyed unhindered communion with the Creator. Their peace and happiness were short-lived, though. When God gave Adam and Eve a simple test of obedience, they failed miserably. Consequently, evil entered into the world, and humanity's intimate communion with God was shattered. Humankind experienced brokenness of the highest order, and all creation suffered from the ill effects of sin. The fall of Adam and Eve subjected humanity to sickness, disease, pain, physical death, and spiritual separation from God. Creation itself also experienced futility and corruption when the human relationship with God was broken.

There was absolutely no hope for humankind if God did not do something Himself. Thankfully, God provided a way in which human beings could have fellowship with Him once again and enjoy the peace that had been lost. He provided a way in which we could be reconciled to Him. Reconciliation repairs the ultimate brokenness of humanity, that of alienation from God. Romans 5:10 declares that we were reconciled to God through the death of His Son. Christ shed His blood on the cross and died in our place for our sins so that we could have eternal life and experience peace with God.

Leviticus 17:11 declares that sin cannot be forgiven without the shedding of blood. The Old Testament requirement for dealing with human sin was animal sacrifice. Under the Old Covenant, priests offered the blood of animals to God as a temporary covering for sin; however, the sacrifice of animals was not a permanent solution to the sin problem. In the New Testament, the blood of Jesus Christ becomes the perfect sacrifice that eradicates the sin problem for all time. My mother wrote a beautiful song about the eternal saving power of the Lord's sacrifice entitled, "The Blood Has Already Been Shed." Several verses from this song read as follows:

The blood has already been shed for you.
The battle has already been fought for you.
The victory has already been won for you,
And Jesus will not die, no, never again.
He said, "Come unto Me if you will live.
All My life to you I freely give.
I am the way, the only way. There's no other way."
Jesus will not die, no, never again.
"Whosoever will may come today.
I am the life and the way."
Yes, the blood has already been shed.[4]

The Savior's sacrificial death on the cross was the only permanent solution for the terrible barrier that existed between a righteous God and sinful humanity. It is wonderful news for humankind *"that God was reconciling the world to Himself in Christ"* (2 Cor. 5:19a).

Because of Jesus' work on the cross, we now have access to God. We can approach God with confidence. We can come into His presence with full assurance that He hears us, that He loves us, and that He will never leave nor forsake us. Our salvation means that we are full members of God's family. Because of the sacrifice of Jesus Christ, we can now cry out to God, "Abba, Father!" Human parents may fail us, but God will never let us down. Psalm 27:10 declares, *"When my father and my mother forsake me, then the Lord will take care of me"* (NKJV). Our position with the Heavenly Father is one of total access.

The Suffering of Jesus Christ Is Vicarious

One thing that makes Jesus' suffering and death so powerful is that He suffered and died in our place. Jesus suffered and died for the sins of the world. Isaiah 53:4 says that Christ *"has borne our griefs and carried our sorrows"* (NKJV). Verse 5 continues:

> But He was wounded for our transgressions, He was bruised for our iniquities; the chastisement for our peace was upon Him, and by His stripes we are healed (NKJV).

Verse 6 declares that "[God] *has laid on* [Christ] *the iniquity of us all"* (NKJV). Second Corinthians 5:21 adds that Christ became a sin offering for us so that we might become the righteousness of God.

These verses speak of Jesus' vicarious suffering and death for humanity. Vicarious suffering is the suffering that one person endures in the place of another. Jesus suffered and died in our place. He took upon Himself the awful consequences of sin so that we could have eternal life. The Lord Jesus Christ laid aside the comforts of Heaven and the privileges of being God in order to become a man (see Phil. 2:5-8). Moreover, He suffered and died a cruel death that He did not deserve, so that we could enjoy a relationship with His Father that we did not deserve. Christ took on our defeat, and He gives us victory. Christ took on our misery, and He gives us joy. Christ took on our sicknesses, and He gives us healing. Christ took on our sin, our pain, our punishment, and our death so that we could take on His eternal life. Jesus' vicarious suffering on the cross has ultimately led to our salvation and wholeness!

> What can wash away my sin?
> Nothing but the blood of Jesus.
> What can make me whole again?
> Nothing but the blood of Jesus.
> O precious is the flow
> That makes me white as snow;
> No other fount I know;
> Nothing but the blood of Jesus.[5]

CRUCIFIED WITH CHRIST

Paul says in Galatians 2:20:

I have been crucified with Christ; it is no longer I who live, but Christ lives in me; and the life which I now live in the flesh I live by faith in the Son of God, who loved me and gave Himself for me (NKJV).

This is similar to what Paul says in Galatians 6:14:

But God forbid that I should boast except in the cross of our Lord Jesus Christ, by whom the world has been crucified to me, and I to the world (NKJV).

These are exciting verses for us because they indicate that we are in union with Jesus Christ. We share in everything that Christ has accomplished. We participate with Christ in every good work the Father ordains. Because we are in Christ and He is in us, every victory He has won belongs to us. Let me give you an example of what I mean.

Some of you reading this book struggle with various types of sin issues like smoking, profanity, or pornography, and you desire to be free from them. If you are not born again (saved), then your first step, of course, is to give your heart to the Lord. You must repent of your sins and ask Jesus Christ to come into your life. If you are born again, then you need to accept the fact that Christ dealt with your sin on the cross. You now are the righteousness of God through Jesus Christ (see 2 Cor. 5:21). Even if you do not feel as if you are the righteousness of God, the Word of God says that you are. Therefore, you must choose to believe what the Word says about you. I am not saying that your sins are an illusion, but I am saying that Christ stripped these sins of their power over you. Put your energy and focus on Christ's victory rather than on the particular sins with which you are struggling.

The Word of God also tells you to reckon yourself dead to sin (see Rom. 6:11). In other words, you must adjust your thinking to the fact that you are dead to sin. When Christ died on the cross, the power of sin over your life died with Him. When Christ rose from the dead, God raised you up with Him to a new life free from the power of sin. Therefore, you need to accept these facts in your heart. When you start to believe and to accept the truth that Christ won your freedom from cigarettes, sexual immorality, profanity, or whatever, it will begin to affect your behavior. You may have to remind yourself each day of your victory in Christ. You may have to fast and pray, but if you do so, you will eventually see this victory manifested in your experience. It would be wise for you to acquire godly accountability partners. These may be Christian counselors, mature friends, pastors, ministry leaders, or support groups. There is no shame in inviting others to help you walk through some of your struggles. The Lord often uses other people to minister to the broken areas of our lives; do not limit Him. Repeat the following:

1. I am reconciled to God.

2. I am a child of God.

3. Christ's victory on the cross was my victory as well.

4. I yield my mind and body to the Lord Jesus Christ.

5. Sin will not rule over me.

6. Sickness will not rule over me.

7. Satan will not rule over me.

8. I renounce the devil and all his works.

9. I am holy and righteous in Christ.

10. I receive the fullness of God's salvation and wholeness in Jesus Christ.

DIVINE EXCHANGE

The cross clearly is a divine instrument of wholeness (see Gal. 3:13). Jesus' work on the cross is what I call a divine exchange. Jesus took all the evil things affecting us and exchanged them for His salvation and eternal life. I would like to lead you in a simple exercise to help you better appreciate what the Lord has done for you. In your mind's eye, picture the Savior experiencing the anguish of the crucifixion. He was beaten; He was tortured; He suffered; and He died on the cross for you. Take a moment to thank Jesus for paying such an awful price for you. Take as long as you need to fellowship with your Lord and Savior.

Now ask the Holy Spirit to apply the power of the cross to your sins, sicknesses, infirmities, pains, weaknesses, hang-ups, and other issues. Imagine that you can place all your concerns and problems into a box. Give the box to Jesus. How does the Lord respond to you? Does He nail the box to the cross? Does the box disappear? Does He incinerate the box? Whatever the response, Jesus certainly wants to exchange your cares and concerns for His peace and rest. By faith, receive the wholeness that God desires to manifest in your life at this very moment. Now thank God for the salvation that He offers to you through Jesus Christ.

I encourage you on a daily basis to go to the cross. Bring your habits to the cross; bring your sins to the cross; bring your guilty conscience to the cross; bring your problems to the cross; bring your weaknesses to the cross. It is time for everything in your life that is not of God to die.

THE RESURRECTION OF JESUS CHRIST

The cross was not the final stop for the Savior. The Lord endured the shame of Calvary and now joyfully sits at the right hand of the throne of God, having secured our salvation (see Heb. 12:2). Between these two states of shame and joy occurred the greatest miracle in human history: the resurrection of the Lord Jesus Christ from the dead. The central claim of the Christian faith is the resurrection. The doctrine of the resurrection asserts that Jesus, having died on the cross, was buried in a tomb, and rose physically from the dead never to return to the grave. Although others have been raised from the dead (e.g., Lazarus in John 11:1-44), the resurrection of Jesus Christ is unique in that He conquered death for all time. We worship a risen Savior who has passed through death and is alive forevermore (see Rev. 1:18).

Matthew, Mark, Luke, and John all record accounts of the resurrection (see Matt. 28:1-20; Mark 16:1-8; Luke 24; John 20–21). In First Corinthians 15:1-2, the apostle Paul declares that the resurrection must be included in the proclamation of the Gospel. Paul then summarizes the good news of salvation in verses 3 and 4:

> For what I received I passed on to you as of first importance: that Christ died for our sins according to the Scriptures, that He was buried, that He was raised on the third day according to the Scriptures.

The resurrection was a historical event attested to by the apostles and over 500 of Christ's followers to whom He appeared before He ascended into Heaven (see verses 5-8). If Jesus did not rise from the dead: (1) preaching is useless; (2) faith is empty; (3) Christianity is untrue; (4) we still are in bondage to sin; and (5) we have no hope (see verses 14-19).

Confession of the Lordship of Christ and belief in His resurrection lead to salvation (see Rom. 10:9). In other words, salvation involves total embrace of the Lord's person and work. As with the crucifixion, the resurrection provides several of salvation's benefits. Two of these are justification and regeneration (see Rom. 4:25; 1 Pet. 1:3). Once again, justification is the process by which God declares us righteous and puts us into right relationship with Himself. Regeneration is spiritual rebirth or re-creation. Jesus spoke of being *"born again"* and Paul stated that the person located in Christ is a *"new creation"* (see John 3:3; 2 Cor. 5:17). We experience new birth and renewal through the power of the Lord's resurrection.

Another benefit of the resurrection of Jesus is that it guarantees us that we too will experience resurrection in the future. All Christians will join our Savior in the experience of eternal, everlasting life (see Rom. 8:1; 1 Cor. 6:14; 2 Cor. 4:14; 1 Thess. 4:14-17). Because we are benefactors of the resurrection, we can look forward to a heavenly inheritance that will never perish, spoil, or fade (see 1 Pet. 1:4).

THE ASCENSION OF JESUS CHRIST

Jesus Christ ascended into Heaven and now sits at the right hand of the Father. Christ's position is:

Far above all principality and power and might and dominion, and every name that is named, not only in this age but also in that which is to come (Ephesians 1:21 NKJV).

In Ephesians 2, Paul reminds us that God raised us to new life in Christ and we sit in heavenly places with Him (verses 4-7). By inference, then, we can conclude that the principalities and powers are under our feet as well. God has placed us in a privileged position of victory over darkness. Although we are not physically in Heaven yet, we share in the Savior's authority over the spirit world.

In order to enable us to walk fully in our delegated authority, God has given us the Holy Spirit. The Holy Spirit is the power that raised Jesus from the dead and caused Him to sit at the right hand of God (see Eph. 1:19-23). This resurrection and ascension power is the same power that works in the church to do immeasurably more than we could ask or imagine (see Eph. 3:20).

The Holy Spirit in our lives is a seal and a guarantee of our wonderful inheritance in Christ, a source of wisdom and revelation, a strengthener, an enabler of prayer, and so much more (see Eph. 1:13-14,17; 3:16,18). Because of the presence and power of the Holy Spirit in us, there is no challenge that we cannot overcome. Ephesians 5:18 commands us to *"be filled with the Spirit."* The Greek literally says, "Be continually and repeatedly filled with the Holy Spirit." In other words, we must surrender to the Spirit's control on a moment-by-moment basis. A believer can never obtain more of the Holy Spirit; however, the Holy Spirit can exercise more control of the life that yields to Him.[6] This control will foster our growth into spiritual adults and will lead us into a daily experience of God's power to overcome evil.

I encourage you each day to thank God for His work of salvation through Christ. Christ died on the cross and rose from the dead for our benefit. We share in His victory over sin, death, and evil. When Christ died, we died. When He rose, we rose with Him. Christ now sits at the right hand of the Father, and we share in His authority and power. Although we eagerly wait for the day when Christ will destroy His enemies, His victory over these principalities and powers is nevertheless a reality in the present. Each day we can accept, celebrate, and appropriate His victory by faith. In Heaven, all of life's problems will be over. However, in my prayer times, I often ask God for a foretaste of Heaven's future reality to manifest in my present experience. As Jesus prayed, *"Your will be done on earth as it is in heaven"* (Matt. 6:10).

UNTITLED POEM

Satan thought that he had won.
He beat and bruised God's precious Son.
But Jesus rose on the third day,
And for the world, He made a way.
Christ conquered sin and death for us.
He nailed our sins onto the cross,
And by His stripes, we are now healed.
The truth to us has been revealed.
We are new creatures, yes indeed.
The work of Christ meets every need,
For wholeness, life, and joy, and peace;
Redeemed by Christ, a sweet release!
God's love is plain for all to see.
His mercy, grace, and gifts are free.
The Holy Spirit fills our cup.
All praise to God! So lift Him up!
In His strength, we overcome!
Rejoice; be glad; the war is won!
Access to God! The veil He tore!
Eternal life forevermore!

—Wilfred Graves Jr.

A PRAYER FOR WHOLENESS IN LIGHT OF THE CROSS, RESURRECTION, AND ASCENSION

Heavenly Father, I bless Your holy name and I praise You for who You are. Thank You for loving me and for sending Your Son, Jesus Christ, to die for my sins on the cross. Thank You, Jesus, for giving Your life. Thank You for shedding Your blood that I might have eternal life. Also, Lord, I thank You for the precious Holy Spirit who lives within me and who strengthens me when I am weak. Holy Spirit, I ask You to take total control of this prayer time. Help me to extinguish pride, to abandon self, and to pray according to the will of the Father.

Heavenly Father, I believe everything the Word says concerning salvation, wholeness, and answered prayer. I rejoice in the decisive victory over sin, sickness, satan, and death that Jesus Christ won at Calvary. All power and authority belong to the Lord. I also recognize, dear God, that I am now vitally connected to Christ in His work at Calvary and beyond. Therefore, I share in His victory, and I have full access to You.

I pray that You will rescue me from the things that diminish or destroy me in my spirit, mind, body, relationships, and other areas of my humanity. Because the stripes of Jesus Christ provide healing and salvation, I ask You, Holy Spirit, to apply to me the benefits of the work of Jesus Christ so that I will receive wholeness. Apply to me the benefits of the life, death, burial, resurrection, ascension, and glorification of Jesus Christ. Also, apply to me the full benefit of Pentecost and any benefits of the second coming that I can now receive.

In fact, I ask that some of the future blessing that awaits me in Heaven come into my present experience as a down payment. There will be no pain, misery, sickness, or death in Heaven. Father, allow me to experience a foretaste of that heavenly reality right now. I now humbly receive everything that You make available to me. Finally, Heavenly Father, I praise You with all my heart. I give You the honor that is Yours alone. In the name of the Lord Jesus Christ, I pray. Amen.

CHAPTER SUMMARY

1. The central theme of preaching is *"Jesus Christ and Him crucified"* (1 Cor. 2:2).

2. Crucifixion was a cruel and degrading form of execution.

3. The death of Jesus on the cross gives us many wonderful benefits.

4. Jesus' suffering and death were vicarious, done in our stead.

5. The resurrection of Jesus Christ is the greatest miracle in human history.

6. God's resurrection and ascension power (i.e., the Holy Spirit) indwells believers.

7. We are united with Christ so that we share in every victory that He won over our enemies.

Reflection/Discussion Questions

1. What new insights did you receive from reading this chapter?

2. What benefits does the cross offer to us?

3. How does the vicarious suffering of Christ encourage you personally?

4. What steps will you take to embrace the message of the cross on a daily basis?

5. Why is the resurrection of Jesus Christ so important to the message of Christianity?

Practical Applications and Activities

1. Tell a family member or friend about what you learned in this chapter.

2. Write a poem or short story about what the cross means to you.

3. Read Numbers 21:4-9 and John 3:14-15. What can you conclude about the connection between the cross and healing from these two passages?

4. Reread the crucifixion and resurrection narratives. Write a letter stating why you are thankful for the death, burial, and resurrection of Jesus Christ.

CHAPTER 4

Holiness and Wholeness

Sin is a clenched fist and its object is the face of God.

—Anonymous

The new birth results in new behavior. Sin and the child of God are incompatible. They may occasionally meet; they cannot live together in harmony.

—John R. W. Stott[1]

THE DANGERS OF SINFUL BEHAVIOR

It is impossible for us to experience wholeness in our lives when we are in bondage to sinful behavior. Sin alienates us from God and prevents us from receiving the fullness of His life, peace, and well-being. God is holy. He is the antithesis of all that is profane or common. Because God is holy, He requires us to live in a manner that reflects His character. He commands us to love others and to conduct ourselves with moral integrity. In order to lead lives that are pleasing to God, we must separate ourselves from sin and walk in holiness. When we play around with sin, when we engage in sexual immorality, when we lie, cheat, and steal, we place ourselves in danger. When we give the devil a foothold, he always takes more than we bargained for, and our lives quickly head for destruction. *"For the wages of sin is death, but the gift of God is eternal life in Christ Jesus our Lord"* (Rom. 6:23). Holiness and righteousness are not old-fashioned or outmoded concepts. Holiness and righteousness actually keep us from many of life's dangers. Is God challenging you to obey His commands with greater faithfulness? These commands are for your good. God loves you and does not want you to get hurt.[2] His holy standards are for His glory and your protection.

The Believer's New Identity in Jesus Christ

In Ephesians 2:1-5, Paul says that believers formerly were dead in trespasses (or transgressions) and sins, but now are alive with Christ. God raised His people from a state of spiritual death, or separation from Him, to a state of spiritual life, or fellowship with Him. The wonderful salvation that Christians now enjoy comes by grace through faith (see Eph. 2:8-9). Grace is God's unmerited favor, His freewill love in action, His unearned blessing, His infinite liberality. Grace is neither a wage nor a reward, but rather a gift. God's grace is completely undeserved by sinful humanity. The acrostic "God's Riches At Christ's Expense" is a helpful reminder of Jesus' sacrifice on the cross. Although grace is free to us, it cost Jesus His very life. The Lord paid the price, and we reap the benefits. The former slave-trader, John Newton, reminds us that God's grace truly is "amazing" indeed:

> Amazing grace, how sweet the sound
> That saved a wretch like me!
> I once was lost, but now am found,
> Was blind but now I see.
> 'Twas grace that taught my heart to fear,
> And grace my fears relieved;
> How precious did that grace appear,
> The hour I first believed![3]

Salvation is by grace through faith. Faith is the human response to God's free and loving gift of salvation in Christ. Faith is unwavering trust in God and continuous dependence on God. We have faith in God because He is the source of all that makes life possible and meaningful. Every good and perfect gift comes from the Heavenly Father (see James 1:17). God has done many good things for us; however, the ultimate act of goodness on His part was the giving of His Son to die on the cross. Faith requires a willingness to surrender to the Lordship of Jesus Christ.

Ephesians 2:10 informs believers of who we are in Christ and what God expects of us as Christians. First, *"We are God's workmanship."* The Greek word *poiema*, translated "workmanship," also translates as "masterpiece," "work of art," or "new creation."[4] God is working out in our lives a marvelous display of His love, glory, power, mercy, and grace. He works on us until our character and actions reflect His own.

The fact that we are God's masterpiece should encourage us greatly. Since we are God's masterpiece, or work of art, then we are very valuable to Him. It does not matter if we are rich or poor, black or white, attractive or unattractive, male or female, educated or uneducated; we all are very special to God. Someone reading this book may not feel particularly special. Maybe you are unhappy with your appearance or your socioeconomic level. Perhaps a physical or mental handicap causes you to experience low self-esteem. I want you to know that God accepts you. Your self-worth derives from your position in Christ rather than from any other consideration. In fact, God loves you just as much as He loves the Lord Jesus Christ Himself (see John 17:23). Think about that! If you are struggling with self-esteem issues, then keep reminding yourself that you are God's masterpiece until the truth of the declaration settles in your spirit and brings joy to your heart.

In addition, we are *"created in Christ Jesus to do good works"* (Eph. 2:10). Good works are the godly character and actions that result from our relationship with Christ and that we accomplish through the power of the Holy Spirit. When we do good works, we lead lives that are pleasing to God, and we become the agents through whom He expresses His divine will in the earth. It is God's will that our character and actions reflect His own. As the Holy Spirit continually transforms us into the image of Christ, our lives will begin to exhibit the characteristics of love, joy, peace, patience, kindness, goodness, self-control, etc. (see Gal. 5:22-23).

Our love for God also will compel us to do good deeds. These good deeds do not cause salvation but will be the result of the salvation that we possess. As the saying goes, "Faith alone saves, but the faith that saves is never alone."[5] Salvation is by grace through faith alone, and if we indeed experience salvation, we will exhibit godly behavior. We will walk in holiness and righteousness because we are a new creation; the old has passed away, and the new has come (see 2 Cor. 5:17). We will love God, our neighbors, and our brothers and sisters in Christ because this is what the Lord requires of us (see 1 John 4:7-11). We will bring healing to the sick, relief to the poor, and liberation to the oppressed because Christ did these things (see Luke 4:18-19).

A good friend of mine, Reverend Timothy Godfrey, conducts worship services each week at a local senior care facility. Each week the residents look forward to his inspirational sermons and uplifting singing. One resident in particular, Viola Black (age 99), calls Tim her spiritual son. Although Tim receives little recognition and no compensation for his regular acts of love and kindness, he nevertheless is a fine example of a Christian servant who is currently doing the good works of Jesus Christ.

The final phrase of Ephesians 2:10 says that the good works that we do are those *"which God prepared in advance for us to do.*" Here, Paul reminds us that we have no reason to boast about the good works that we do because God Himself made these works possible. God works through Christ to empower us for His service. God is the source of our life, strength, and good works. We can do nothing of value without Him.

HOLINESS AND WHOLENESS IN THE CHRISTIAN COMMUNITY: EPHESIANS 4:17-32

In Ephesians 4:17-24, the apostle exhorts his readers to abandon their former sinful practices and to embrace lifestyles of holiness and righteousness that evidence the new life that they have in Jesus Christ.[6] The unregenerate self is like dirty clothing. We remove dirty clothing before cleansing can occur, and then we put on fresh clothing. Paul's readers are to forsake the sins of the past and to receive a renewal of their minds and spirits (see verses 22-24).[7] This shift in mentality can only occur through the strength and power of the Holy Spirit, acting on the human mind and spirit (see Eph. 3:16; Titus 3:5). Paul says in Galatians 5:16, "*Live by the Spirit, and you will not gratify the desires of the sinful nature.*" The Spirit of God enables us to think godly thoughts and to lead godly lives. The work of the Holy Spirit is a continual process that allows believers to become in reality what God created us to be in Christ.

Verses 25-32 include a list of relational vices and virtues that belong respectively to the old and new lives. Paul replaces each bad vice with a good virtue that will promote unity and strengthen relationships: truth replaces lying (see Eph. 4:25); reconciliation replaces unrestrained anger (4:26); hard work and generosity replace stealing (4:28); helpful words replace harmful ones (4:29); compassion and forgiveness replace bitterness, passion, anger, and insults (4:31-32).[8]

Verse 25 condemns falsehood, that which is untrue (see also Col. 3:9-10). When Christians lie to one another, they injure fellowship and hinder the proper functioning of the body. There can be no real growth, unity, progress, or trust when dishonesty is present in the community. The inevitable result of falsehood is distrust and hurt feelings.

Paul directs his second exhortation at anger (see Eph. 4:26-27).[9] We all become angry at times, but we should not allow our anger to degenerate into sin. Anger blocks clarity of thought and objectivity. It can hinder us from doing the things of which God approves (see James 1:20). We may get angry for legitimate reasons. Yet, we must control our emotions and seek God for wisdom instead of allowing anger to continue for long periods. Unchecked anger allows the enemy access to our lives. He can foster pride, self-righteousness, bitterness, hatred, strife, and revenge in us if we are not careful. These sins are devastating to our personal relationships.

Ephesians 4:28 addresses the issue of stealing. Stealing is an attempt to get something for nothing.[10] Because God commands honest hard work, stealing is never an option for us. We must give up stealing and develop hearts of generosity. Not only should we seek to provide for our own needs, but we also should seek to care for those who are less fortunate than we are. During a recent Sunday service, our local church congregation responded to the severe financial need of one of our members. Without prompting, a single individual was moved to share a small sum with the one in need. Within seconds, hundreds of others formed a line to share of their resources as well. It was a beautiful picture of love, spiritual sensitivity, and Christian generosity. God desires to use His people as instruments of love and channels of blessing.

Paul's fourth warning is against unwholesome speech (see verse 29). The word *unwholesome* literally means "rotten."[11] Rotten words such as gossip injure others and create division. Christians are not to speak rotten words, but rather words that are gracious and helpful (see also Eccles. 10:12; Col. 4:6).[12]

In verse 30, Paul reminds his readers that they are sealed with the Holy Spirit (see Eph. 1:13-14). The Spirit's presence should motivate us to rid ourselves of bitterness, rage, anger, brawling, slander, and every form of malice (see verse 31). Instead of harboring these characteristics, we must *"be kind and compassionate to one another, forgiving each other, just as in Christ God forgave you"* (verse 32). Wholeness in personal relationships starts with kind and gracious words and godly actions (see also Col. 3:12-17).

HOLINESS AND SEXUAL WHOLENESS: EPHESIANS 5:3-7

Paul continues his discussion of morality and ethics in Ephesians 5:3-7. Paul declares in verse 3:

> *But among you there must not be even a hint of sexual immorality, or of any kind of impurity, or of greed, because these are improper for God's holy people.*

Paul's warning is of special relevance today in our society where morality is on the decline and selfish pursuit of pleasure is on the rise. Sexual immorality, impurity, and greed are perversions of love. They are inconsistent with God's standard of holiness and improper for the child of God. "Sexual immorality" or "fornication" (NKJV) comes from the Greek word *porneia*, from which we derive the word *pornography*. *Porneia* refers to all forms of illegitimate and ungodly sexual union, such as prostitution, fornication, adultery, promiscuity, same-sex intercourse, and bestiality.[13] Related closely to the idea of *porneia* is that of impurity. Impurity refers to different types of sexual perversion. Greed or covetousness (NKJV) in this passage refers to unrestrained sexual appetite that treats other people as objects for one's own gratification. Paul's admonitions in verse 3 are similar to those found in First Thessalonians 4:3-8.

97

The issue of sexual immorality is not only a physical issue; it is a mental one as well. Jesus said in Matthew 5:27-28:

You have heard that it was said, "Do not commit adultery." But I tell you that anyone who looks at a woman lustfully has already committed adultery with her in his heart.

Sin begins with a thought before it translates into an action. This is why pornography is so destructive. Pornography refers to sexually explicit material intended to produce sexual arousal. This material includes images and writings available in magazines, books, and films, on the Internet, and even on cell phones. Some of today's popular music actually is pornographic in its effect on listeners. Pornography desensitizes the mind and opens the door to other sins, such as rape and child molestation. Pornography degrades women in particular and reduces sex to an athletic event devoid of intimacy and the love of God. Pornography assaults the image of God in both men and women and ruins many marriages. It creates an unrealistic view of the frequency of sex and portrays perverted acts as normal or acceptable. Pornography is satanically inspired and demonically empowered. If you are using pornography in any form, stop it immediately. Your bondage will only increase as you continue to give the enemy access to your thought life.[14]

Peter Michaels learned the hard away about the perils of sexual sin. Peter grew up in a Christian home and made a commitment to Christ during his early teens while attending a church summer camp. His parents taught him to abstain from sexual involvement until marriage; however, he did maintain a healthy interest in the opposite sex during adolescence. Peter dated in high school and always treated young women with great respect. He often wondered, though, whether his virginity made him less of a man than some of his peers were.

While Peter was a sophomore in college, a friend introduced him to pornography, which he continued to view occasionally throughout his 20s. Peter always felt that the use of this explicit material was wrong, but he became addicted to the thrill of seeing naked bodies and entering into a world of sexual fantasy. Peter often would utilize pornography to aid him in masturbation. The practice soon became a compulsive habit.

When Peter entered into his late 20s, he discovered that the thrill that he once received from the use of pornography had diminished significantly, so he began to search for riskier, more stimulating sexual activity. He started to frequent a seedy massage parlor in the red-light district of town where he typically would receive much more than massages. The women would allow Michael to fondle them. Sometimes they also would stimulate him manually or orally for financial compensation. Peter soon graduated from these places and began to visit prostitutes. He truly was on a downward spiritual, emotional, and moral spiral that did not end until he eventually was arrested in a police prostitution sting. Peter has since recommitted himself to the Lord, but not before enduring a considerable amount of shame, brokenness, and emotional pain. Peter long ago should have surrendered his sex drive to God and allowed God to lead him down a pathway of legitimate sexual fulfillment.

Michelle Peters grew up in a very strict Christian home with no sports, no movies, no dancing, no amusement parks, and no dating. Her parents were ministers in a nondenominational church that taught a rigid separation from all "worldly" activities and required members to attend church excessively. Michelle was conscientious, studious, and well behaved as a child and a teenager, but she secretly began to resent the religion of her parents during her senior year of high school.

When Michelle left home for college, she eagerly embraced the freedom and "fun" of being on her own. She could now escape the oppressive rules and regulations of her parents and her church. As a freshman, she had her first drink of alcohol at a campus party, experimented with marijuana with her roommate, and lost her virginity to a popular football player.

Michelle truly enjoyed physical intimacy and found herself in numerous sexual encounters while in college. After a while, though, these encounters did not thrill her as much as they once did. Michelle often felt cheap, empty, and even used. "These men don't really care about me," she said to herself. "They only care about my body." Michelle began to crave genuine love, commitment, and companionship, but all she knew was sex.

After Michelle graduated from college, she moved to a new city and decided to reconnect with church. She soon met a loving Christian man, and she is now happily married with three children. The fulfillment of companionship for which she sought in college has now become a reality. "How could I have ever settled for anything less than this?" she often asks herself. "I never found true satisfaction until I did things God's way!"

God's holy alternative to sexual immorality and impurity is a healthy marriage (see Prov. 5:18-20; 1 Cor. 7:1-9; Heb. 13:4). Marriage between a man and a woman is the only context for sexual expression that God sanctions. The single person will never derive sexual fulfillment from pornography, compulsive masturbation, sexual toys, or promiscuity.[15] He or she will only find sexual fulfillment in a loving, committed marriage relationship. Yet, even in marriage, God requires sexual purity and self-control. Sex within marriage should glorify God and draw husbands and wives closer to God and to one another. Love must be the guiding principle behind all sexual involvement. When we love others, we will never treat them with disrespect or use them merely to gratify our own evil desires. On the contrary, we will respect them and treat them in ways that will please the Heavenly Father. Love values other people; it does not see them simply as objects of pleasure. Love is patient; love is kind; love is not self-seeking (see 1 Cor. 13:4-5). Love always has the highest good in mind for others.

Finally, never forget that your body is the temple of the Holy Spirit (see 1 Cor. 6:18-19). It was not made for sexual immorality, but for the Lord (see 1 Cor. 6:13). Before you engage in sexual activity of any kind, take a moment to acknowledge the Lord and to commit yourself to His holy standards. Sex is a beautiful gift that can bring great fulfillment to men and women as they follow the loving prescriptions of the Creator.

Paul declares in Ephesians 5:4, *"Nor should there be obscenity, foolish talk or coarse joking, which are out of place, but rather thanksgiving."* "Obscenity" includes profanity and all talk that is shameful.[16] "Foolish talk" refers to words lacking decency or respectability. "Coarse joking" refers to crude humor, dirty insinuations, and double entendres—any type of so-called clever speech that borders on the improper. Instead of using improper speech, Christians should fill their mouths with "thanksgiving." We should replace all locker room humor with holy speech and with sincere appreciation for the beautiful gift of sex to the marriage relationship. We should never allow improper speech to compete with our thanksgiving and praise to God.

Paul continues in verse 5: "No *immoral, impure or greedy person—such a man is an idolater—has any inheritance in the kingdom of Christ and of God."*

In every generation, there will be those who make light of sin and ridicule God's standards of holiness and righteousness. We have all heard the following excuse: "Well, God knows that I have needs. After all, I am free in Christ and there is nothing wrong with a little fun! I am not hurting anybody." Do not entertain such false reasoning. Christ does not give us freedom *to* sin; Christ offers us freedom *from* sin.

Paul writes in Romans 6:1-2: *"Shall we continue in sin that grace may abound? Certainly not! How shall we who died to sin live any longer in it?"*(NKJV).

One young fellow who thought that he could get around God's clear sexual standards said with brazenness, "No, we are not married, and yes, we are having sex, but we are both Christians, and two clean sheets cannot dirty each other." My response is that even though two clean sheets cannot dirty each other, they can certainly wrinkle each other, and Jesus Christ is looking for a holy church without spot or wrinkle or any such thing. Clearly, this young man was no Bible scholar.

Paul equates sexual immorality with idolatry. When people engage in sexual immorality, their sexual passions begin to dominate their lives and divert their attention away from the Lord. These people soon become greedy or covetous, making a god of what they seek to possess. Immorality, impurity, and greed exclude a person from inheritance in the Kingdom of Christ and God. As Paul says in First Corinthians 6:9-11:

> *Do not be deceived: Neither the sexually immoral nor idolaters nor adulterers nor male prostitutes nor homosexual offenders nor thieves nor the greedy nor drunkards nor slanderers nor swindlers will inherit the kingdom of God. And that is what some of you were. But you were washed, you were sanctified, you were justified in the name of the Lord Jesus Christ and by the Spirit of our God.*

Although God's Kingdom is denied to those who practice immoral behavior, Paul is not saying that the believer who makes a mistake and commits one of these sins is automatically excluded from God's Kingdom. What Paul is saying is that sexual immorality, impurity, and covetousness characterize the lifestyles of those outside the Kingdom of Christ and God. If you are reading this book and you are in bondage to sexual sin, then there is hope for you. Jesus Christ can set you free and *"if the Son makes you free, you shall be free indeed"* (John 8:36 NKJV).

First, turn to the Lord in repentance and submission and ask Him to cleanse you of sin and fill you with His Spirit. Second, ask the Lord to give you a proper view of sex and a respect both for yourself and for others. Third, ask God Himself to meet your needs. Sometimes people engage in sexual activity to fill the voids in their lives; however, God Himself is the only source of genuine, lasting fulfillment. Pornography, masturbation, and sexual promiscuity cannot comfort us. God is our only true source of comfort, and we will never be happy until we do things His way. Fourth, you must begin to concentrate on things that will lead to holy living. As Paul says in Philippians 4:8:

> *Whatever is true, whatever is noble, whatever is right, whatever is pure, whatever is lovely, whatever is admirable— if anything is excellent or praiseworthy—think about such things.*

Finally, I would like to encourage you to find several strong Christians to whom you can be accountable. Ecclesiastes 4:10 declares: *"If one falls down, his friend can help him up. But pity the man who falls and has no one to help him up!"*

Let us help one another to walk in victory by holding our brothers and sisters accountable.

LIES THAT HINDER WHOLENESS

Human beings are very good at self-deception. We can justify almost anything if we let our guards down. I would like to expose a few lies that will hinder you in your journey toward wholeness.

Are you guilty of any of these false beliefs? If you are, then I challenge you to allow God to renew your thinking. It takes courage to admit when we are on a pathway to personal destruction; however, God's truth can set us free from the bondage of sin.

- *Lie #1:* I cannot relinquish control of this one area of my life to God. He will let me slide because I am trying hard to be a good person.

- *Truth #1:* If Jesus Christ does not control every area of your life, then you really have not made Him Lord of your life. God requires total surrender to His will and complete obedience to His commands. He will never adjust His holy requirements to faulty human reasoning.

- *Lie #2:* Everyone else is doing it. It is unrealistic to think that anyone can follow the archaic rules of the Bible. After all, this is the 21st century.

- *Truth #2:* God gave His Word for all people at all times. His requirements are eternally relevant.

- *Lie #3:* Since I am already living in sin, I might as well enjoy it.

- *Truth #3: "The wages of sin is death"* (Rom. 6:23). If you find yourself in sin's grasp, get out of it immediately. Any "enjoyment" that results from sinful activity is temporary at best and illusory at worse. Sin inevitably will destroy you, if not in this life, then certainly in the next.

- *Lie #4:* I am not out of control; I can stop this behavior at any time.

- *Truth #4:* If you were in control, then you would have stopped the behavior long ago.

- *Lie #5:* I need this _____ (crutch, substance, relationship, etc.) to survive.

- *Truth #5:* God always has a holy and righteous alternative to the destructive things that you embrace in life. Why should you settle for less than God's best?

- *Lie #6:* I will do better as soon as my life situation changes.

- *Truth #6:* Procrastination is never good. Turn to God right now. If you think that you will change tomorrow, tomorrow never arrives.

- *Lie #7:* I can play with fire without being burned. I can entertain sin without participating in it. I can overcome sin without cutting access to it.

- *Truth #7:* How many unwanted pregnancies have resulted from this faulty reasoning? Do not underestimate your susceptibility to sin. Wisdom requires the avoidance of sin at all costs.

- *Lie #8:* I do not have any other options. I do not have a choice. I must do the wrong thing.

- *Truth #8:* "The right thing" is always an option and the best choice. Doing the right thing can seem difficult, but God will bless you when you do things His way.

- *Lie #9:* I can pray my way out of the negative consequences of my bad decisions.

- *Truth #9:* God is gracious; however, oftentimes we must suffer the consequences of our actions. Therefore, it is best to make the wisest choices possible.

- *Lie #10:* I am not hurting anyone else.

- *Truth #10:* You are injuring your relationship with God by engaging in sin. You also are hurting yourself. Sinful actions have a negative effect on your character.

- *Lie #11:* I said that I am sorry, so I am now right with God.

- *Truth #11:* Repentance is not "I am sorry that I got caught" or "I am sorry that I am suffering the consequences of my actions." Repentance is coming into agreement with God in our hearts that something is wrong. We must take personal responsibility for our thoughts and actions. We must confess God's perspective and make a choice to do things God's way with His help.

Surrender to the Lord

It is time for the people of God to get serious about the avoidance of sin. We cannot resist the devil while playing around on his territory. Sin is a hindrance to wholeness. In order to enjoy victory in life, we must surrender to the Lord. We sing in our churches:

> All to Jesus, I surrender; all to Him I freely give;
> I will ever love and trust Him,
> In His presence freely live.
> All to Jesus I surrender, Lord I give myself to Thee;
> Fill me with Thy love and power;
> Let Thy blessing fall on me.
> I surrender all, I surrender all,
> All to Thee, my blessed Savior, I surrender all.[17]

Only when we surrender ourselves to the supreme Lordship of Christ will we become effective witnesses to the world. Only when we surrender to His Lordship will we become rivers of life that splash God's presence onto those in need of salvation. Only when we surrender to the supreme Lordship of Jesus Christ can we truly say that we are His representatives. The one who surrenders himself or herself to the supreme Lordship of Jesus Christ is the one who can pray with sincerity, "Not my will, but Yours be done." The one who surrenders to Christ is a person of prayer, a person of the Word, a person who walks in loving obedience to God, and a person who is sensitive to the Holy Spirit. Surrender to the Lord requires a renewed mind and a humble heart, turning away from sin and turning to God, putting off the old self and putting on the new self. The one who surrenders to Jesus Christ is the one who allows the fruit of the Spirit to grow in his or her life. A surrendered life is one that overflows with love and reverence for God and love and concern for our brothers and sisters in Christ. A surrendered life is one that is committed to God with no strings attached. I encourage you to surrender yourself to the supreme Lordship of Jesus Christ.

DEALING WITH INWARD ENTICEMENTS TO SIN

In this section, I would like to offer some practical advice on dealing with inward enticements to sin. First, do not ever forget that the Lord Jesus Christ is on your side. He is your Savior and your Advocate (i.e., the one who defends you) with the Father (see 1 John 2:1-2). He is a faithful High Priest who has been tempted in every point, yet without sin (see Heb. 4:14-16). Because the Lord Jesus Christ can relate to you in your temptations, the Heavenly Father certainly will give you a sympathetic ear. He also will provide you with the wisdom and grace to deal with your temptations when you call on Him (see James 1:5-8; 1 Cor. 10:13).

Second, because Jesus Christ is your Savior, you have been baptized into His body by the Holy Spirit who now lives within you (see 1 Cor. 12:13; Rom. 8:8-9). The Holy Spirit is a Comforter, Counselor, Strengthener, and Standby. Since He now lives within you, you consciously can choose not to sin (see Rom. 6:12-14). You can flee sinful desires and aggressively pursue righteousness (see 2 Tim. 2:22). You also can see spiritual fruit develop in your life (see Gal. 5:16-26).

Third, you should not minimize the importance of prayer, Scripture reading, and fasting. When you draw close to God in prayer, He draws close to you. When you read and meditate on God's Word daily, it renews your mind (see Ps. 119:9-11; Rom. 12:1-2). Fasting can be an effective method of surrender to the Lord (see Esther 4:16; Isa. 58; Matt. 4:2; 6:16-18).[18] A simple fast could consist of skipping one or more meals and spending the time in prayer and Scripture reading rather than eating.

Typically, near the beginning of each year, I enter into a special period of consecration (usually 40 days) to the Lord. Each day, I fast until noon or later and spend several hours in prayer, Bible reading, and worship. These extended times with God are usually occasioned by tremendous mental clarity and a greater awareness of His presence and power. I also have experienced major spiritual victories in my life during some of these times of consecration. I challenge you to find every opportunity that you can to spend time with the Lord. He desires for you to grow in your relationship with Him.

Fourth, always surround yourself with people who can help you to do the right things (see Eccles. 4:9-12). The adage, "There is strength in numbers," is certainly true when those numbers consist of godly individuals. Obey the words of James 5:16 by confessing your sins and weaknesses to brothers and sisters in the Lord. Accountability is good for the soul and can be a source of healing and restoration (see Gal. 6:1-2).

Fifth, although you cannot avoid all temptations, you certainly can avoid some of them through the exercise of wisdom. If, for example, you are sensitive to gratuitous sex scenes in movies, then you should not watch sexually explicit material or any material that has the possibility of becoming sexually explicit. If you have a weakness for Internet pornography, then place a filter on your computer.

Do not set yourself up to sin. Minimize your access to sin as much as possible and clothe yourself with Christ (see Rom. 13:12-14).

Sixth, if you cannot seem to escape the grasp of a particular temptation, then you should examine your heart to determine if you are seeking counterfeit fulfillment from the sin when God Himself has provided the genuine source of fulfillment. For example, if you are using drugs or alcohol to deal with pain or to gain a false sense of joy, then you should turn to God, whose peace transcends human understanding (see Phil. 4:6-7) and in whose presence is fullness of joy (see Ps. 16:11). God always has a better and righteous alternative to sin. You need to do things His way. Only then will you be truly happy.

Finally, you must be alert, self-controlled, and prepared, for as First Peter 5:8b declares, *"Your enemy the devil prowls around like a roaring lion looking for someone to devour."* Commit yourself to consistent and aggressive obedience to God, building your faith during the good times, so that when temptations do come, you will have the strength to overcome them. Do not be caught off guard.

There may be a reader of this chapter who feels trapped by the grip of sin. Perhaps you are suffering from compulsive behavior or the unusual sense of demonic harassment and intimidation. If this describes you, then you may be a candidate for deliverance ministry. I recommend that you consult someone with experience in this area.[19] You also need to join a God-fearing, Christ-honoring, Spirit-filled church where you will receive spiritual and emotional support and instruction in the Word of God.

Each day, you should reaffirm your faith in Jesus Christ and commit yourself to personal holiness. Renounce, forsake, abandon, and turn away from the sins of your past, the sins of your family line, or the sins of any group with which you are associated or connected. Ask God to break the power of sin over you, your family, your loved ones, the nation, etc. Also, make a conscious effort to forgive those who have hurt you in the past. Pray for the offenders. Make a choice to love them. Ask God to save, deliver, bless, and prosper them and to bring healing and reconciliation if this is possible. Even if reconciliation is not possible, you must release the emotional and spiritual poison of unforgiveness. Commit yourself to the Lordship of Jesus Christ and ask Him to fill you with the Holy Spirit. Welcome the operation of the Spirit in your life and ask Him to apply the full benefit of Christ's redemption to your spirit, mind, and body.

Resist the devil and his evil forces. Command any dark forces attacking you to leave your presence by the authority of Jesus Christ. They must flee according to the truth of Scripture (see James 4:7). Finally, continue to commit yourself daily to the Lord in prayer and Bible study. You also must meet consistently with other mature believers. Join a Bible study, home cell group, Sunday school, or other fellowship group. Healthy relationships promote individual wholeness. Involve yourself with a church family that will love and support you.

A Prayer of Commitment and Surrender to God

Heavenly Father, I humble myself in worship before You. You are worthy of glory, honor, and praise. You are infinite in grace, rich in mercy, and liberal in compassion. I also thank You for the gift of Your Son, Jesus Christ. Jesus Christ is my Lord and Savior; He is my Deliverer, Healer, and Redeemer. He is the one who brings blessing and transformation into my life. He is my all in all. Thank You, Jesus, for shedding Your precious blood that I might have eternal life. Thank You also for the Holy Spirit, who makes me more like You. Holy Spirit, fill my life with love, joy, peace, patience, gentleness, goodness, faithfulness, meekness, and self-control.

Father, I ask You to show me the areas of my life that displease You. Free me from deception of every kind. Sanctify me with Your truth; Your Word is truth. Reveal to me any area in which the enemy has gotten a stronghold, a foothold, or even a toehold. I want to be clean; I want to be saved; I want to be whole; and I certainly want to be free. Dear God, I receive the freedom that You offer to me right now. I turn away from sin, and I turn toward You. I repent of the things in my life that are displeasing to You. Free me from the control of sinful thoughts, corrupt speech, and ungodly actions. [At this point, repent of any specific sins that God brings to your mind. Some possibilities include idolatry, rebellion, unforgiveness, bitterness, sexual immorality, pride, greed, and disobedience.]

Father, I yield myself to Your will. I cast down imaginations and every high thing that exalts itself against the knowledge of God and bring every thought into captivity to the obedience of Christ. I also present my body to You as a living sacrifice and spiritual act of worship. I declare that my body is a temple of the Holy Spirit, and I dedicate myself to righteousness, holiness, and godliness.

Dear God, I need the Spirit of wisdom and revelation in the knowledge of You. I need to know You better. I desire an intimate relationship with You. I want to commune with You daily and keep in step with Your Spirit. Help me to see how great You are and to appreciate what I have in Christ. I am complete in Christ (see Col. 2:10). I am accepted in the Beloved (see Eph. 1:6). I have the resurrection and ascension power of Jesus Christ within me (see Eph. 1:19-23). *I can do and endure all things through Christ who strengthens me* (see Phil. 4:13).

The Lord Jesus Christ sits in heavenly places above the principalities and powers (see Eph. 1:19-23). *I also recognize that Christ has disarmed, stripped, and humiliated these powers* (see Col. 2:15). *Therefore, I take my rightful place of authority in relationship to these forces. I stand against the enemy and resist his assaults against my mind, body, family, relationships, finances, possessions, dreams, pursuits, and all other concerns. I praise God for the protection of the cross and the blood of Jesus Christ. By the authority of the Word of God, the dark forces of the enemy must flee. Any evil spirits that have attached themselves to my life and are causing fear, anger, sickness, sexual compulsion, etc., I command you to leave my presence and to go to the place where the Lord Jesus Christ sends you.*

Father, I give my mind and my emotions to You, and I reject anything that seeks to weaken my relationship with You. I commit myself to a life of integrity, purity, and holiness and I will refrain from taking ungodly shortcuts. I also reckon myself dead to sin, but alive unto God through Jesus Christ (see Rom. 6:11). *I do not have to obey evil impulses because I am dead to sin. I have the authority and power to resist the enemy because I am dead to sin. I submit to the Living Word (i.e., Jesus Christ); I will obey the written Word; and I will use the spoken Word under the power of the Holy Spirit. Allow Your Word, O God, to become a part of me. Allow Your Word to renew my mind, strengthen my body, and quicken my spirit.*

Dear God, once again, I declare my loving surrender to You. I put off the old man and I put on the new man (see Eph. 4:22-24). *I put off selfishness and sin, and I put on Jesus Christ.*

"I have been crucified with Christ. I don't live any longer. Christ lives in me. My faith in the Son of God helps me to live my life in my body. He loved me. He gave Himself for me" (Galatians 2:20).[20]

Holy Spirit, I ask You to apply to me the full benefit of the life, death, burial, resurrection, ascension, and glorification of Jesus Christ. Help me to walk in the full victory, freedom, and power of Pentecost and to receive every provision that Heaven has to offer. O God, I want the fullness of Your presence and Your power to manifest in my life today.

Father, order my steps today and help me to receive Your wisdom and Your direction. Also, help me to yield to the leading of Your Spirit in every aspect of my life. I enter into this day with faith, confidence, and trust. I ask You to help me where I am deficient and protect me from the evil one. I reaffirm my commitment to You and to Your will. I also will walk in obedience to Your Word. When I make mistakes, I ask You to help me to see the error of my ways and to get back on course immediately.

Finally, Father, I surrender to Your plans and purposes for my life. I accept Your vision for my life, vocation, and pursuits. I want to be all that You have created me to be. I acknowledge that Your way is the best way. I joyfully accept Your best for my life and I thank You for what You have done for, in, and through me and for what You will continue to do for, in, and through me. In the name of the Lord Jesus Christ, I pray. Amen.

Chapter Summary

1. Because God is holy, He requires His children to pursue holiness.

2. Holiness is a state of separation from sin or ungodliness.

3. Christians are to pursue unity with other believers and to refrain from activities that will harm one another.

4. Christians are to pursue sexual purity in their thoughts, speech, and actions.

5. Holy living pleases the Father and protects us from all kinds of harm.

REFLECTION/DISCUSSION QUESTIONS

1. What new insights did you receive from reading this chapter?

2. What is holiness?

3. What are some of the specific sins addressed in this chapter? Are you guilty of any of these sins?

4. How does sin affect our pursuit of wholeness?

5. In what ways will you guard against sin?

6. What advice would you give to a person dealing with sexual temptation?

Practical Applications and Activities

1. Record in a journal any sin areas that you need to surrender to God.

2. Tell a family member or friend about what you learned in this chapter.

3. Write out your own prayer of repentance and dedication to the Lord.

4. Discuss your struggles with someone who will hold you accountable to your Christian commitments.

CHAPTER 5

The Secret of a Carefree Life

Worry affects circulation, the heart, the glands, the whole nervous system. I have never known a man who died from overwork, but many who died from doubt.

—Charles H. Mayo: American Mercury[1]

If I can stop one heart from breaking,
I shall not live in vain:
If I can ease one life the aching,
or cool one pain,
Or help one fainting robin
unto his nest again,
I shall not live in vain.

—Emily Dickinson[2]

Do not be afraid of tomorrow, for God is already there.

—Anonymous

EMOTIONAL PROTECTION AGAINST WORRY, FEAR, AND EMOTIONAL DISTRESS

God cares for the emotional health and well-being of His children. In fact, He desires for us to be carefree. The carefree person is someone who is free from worry. The carefree Christian, although he or she may be caught in a raging storm, experiences God's peace in the middle of the storm. We all go through storms in life. Some things are common to the human experience. One of the many battles that we all face is the emotional one. Our emotions can be up one minute and down the next. One moment we are on a mountaintop of promise and hope; the next moment we are in a valley of despair and hopelessness.

The main emotional issue I wish to address at this time is the issue of worry. Human beings are well acquainted with worry. In fact, some of you reading this chapter may have perfected the art of worry. It seems that life presents us with a myriad of opportunities to experience worry, fear, and emotional distress.

Sometimes we worry about our job security and finances. We must feed, clothe, and house our families and ourselves, but we continually face the uncertainty that comes from an unstable economy. For so many of us, the economic realities of life become a tool used by satan to foster fear in our lives and create tension in our relationships, especially our marital relationships. How quickly we forget the words of Jesus in Matthew 6:31-33, where He says:

> *Therefore do not worry, saying, "What shall we eat?" or "What shall we drink?" or "What shall we wear?"...For your heavenly Father knows that you need all these things. But seek first the kingdom of God and His righteousness, and all these things shall be added to you* (NKJV).

The Lord is greater than the economy, and He will supply all our needs according to His riches in glory by Christ Jesus (see Phil. 4:19). God's promise to take care of us does not remove our responsibility to make sound financial decisions for ourselves, but it does mean that God is ultimately the Provider. He is Yahweh-jireh, the God who provides. He is the God who makes a way out of no way. He is the God who speaks to nothing and says, "Let there be." Hagar will tell you that God can create a well of water in the middle of a scorching desert. Sarah and Hannah will testify that God can breathe life into a barren womb. Abraham and Isaac will attest to the fact that God will provide a sacrificial lamb just in time. The children of Israel saw firsthand that God could rain manna out of Heaven to fulfill dietary needs. Elijah learned that God would command the birds to feed His children if necessary. Our God is a provider, and He has infinitely many ways to bless us. Therefore, we really have nothing about which to worry.

Another main cause of worry for many people is the fear of death. Shortly after the September 11 tragedy in 2001, I read an issue of *Time Magazine* entitled, "The Fear Factor." The bulk of the magazine's almost 100 pages highlighted some of the threats that had terrorized Americans since that infamous day in September: threats such as bioterrorism, nuclear weapons, and al-Qaeda training camps on American soil. Now it seems that every time we turn on our television sets to watch the news, images of misery, bloodshed, and chaos bombard us on a continual basis. For many of us, the threats of terrorism, war, violence, and disease overwhelm our imaginations, and for some of us, the fear of death prevents us from really enjoying life.

We do not have to fear death, though. The Lord Jesus Christ conquered death at Calvary and stripped it of its power. Jesus Christ defeated satan, marched him naked through the streets (see Col. 2:15 MSG),[3] and rescued us from ultimate destruction. Christians have a blessed hope and look forward to the day when God Himself will:

> *Wipe away every tear from* [our] *eyes;* [a day when] *there shall be no more death, nor sorrow, nor crying... * [and] *no more pain...* (Revelation 21:4 NKJV).

With such a glorious future, we really should not fear or worry about death because death is just a temporary foe.

The enemy wants the people of God to worry and to become fearful. He wants us to become physically ill and literally worry ourselves to death. Worry can trigger a number of adverse physical effects. When we allow fear to get a hold of our minds, it takes on a life of its own. It becomes a brutal and crippling type of enslavement.

Many of you who are reading this book are on the brink of despair. Because of your finances or your health or your circumstances or for some other reason, worry and fear have entered your life and locked you into an emotional prison, but I challenge you today under the power of the Holy Spirit to come out of it. Come out of that emotional prison in the name of the Lord Jesus Christ. Whom the Son sets free is free indeed, and where the Spirit of the Lord is, there is freedom (see John 8:36; 2 Cor. 3:17). God has not given you *a spirit of fear, but of power and of love and of a sound mind"* (2 Tim. 1:7 NKJV).

First Peter 5:7 captures the secret of a carefree life quite beautifully. The verse reads, *"Casting all your care upon Him, for He cares for you"* (NKJV). The words of the apostle in First Peter 5:7 are similar to those of the psalmist in Psalm 55:22. There, David exhorts God's people to *"Cast your burden on the Lord, and He shall sustain you; He shall never permit the righteous to be moved"* (NKJV). The believer must release the weight and the bondage of worry into the capable and supportive hands of God, whose sustaining power and loving concern is available to all His children. The privilege that God extends to us to cast our cares upon Him, to be carefree, is one of the many facets of His grace.

The Christians to whom Peter writes had countless opportunities to worry. They had many natural reasons for fear, anxiety, and emotional distress. They were going through great persecution and trials. They were suffering tremendously because of their commitment to Jesus Christ and the principles of righteousness (e.g., see 1 Pet. 3:13-17). The apostle addressed these concerns, writing:

Beloved, do not think it strange concerning the fiery trial which is to try you... but rejoice to the extent that you partake of Christ's sufferings, that when His glory is revealed, you may also be glad with exceeding joy (1 Peter 4:12-13 NKJV).

Even Peter himself had many opportunities to worry. He was living during a time when Christianity was in its infancy—a time of tremendous opposition, a time of incredible persecution, a time of martyrdom, or dying for the faith. Peter more than likely wrote his epistle shortly before his death, a death that history tells us was by crucifixion. Yet, despite the reality of persecution and suffering, and even with his own death imminent, Peter tells his readers, *"Casting all your care upon Him, for He cares for you"* (1 Pet. 5:7 NKJV).

Now, what does it mean to cast our cares upon the Lord? To cast our cares upon the Lord means to hurl them upon Him or to throw them upon Him. The act of casting our cares upon the Lord is a decisive act of the will. We must decide to do it. We should pray, "God, I refuse to carry this burden of fear and worry any longer. You take it! You can handle this. I place my worries into Your capable hands. Your mighty hands are big enough and strong enough to carry my burdens. I cast every care and concern upon You."

Casting our cares upon the Lord requires trust. The trust displayed by Shadrach, Meshach, and Abed-Nego as they faced Nebuchadnezzar in Daniel 3 truly inspires me. King Nebuchadnezzar threatened to throw these young men into a blazing furnace because they refused to worship an idol that he had erected. In Daniel 3:17-18, the three Hebrew boys responded to the king:

If we are thrown into the blazing furnace, the God we serve is able to save us from it...But even if He does not,

121

we want you to know, O king, that we will not serve your
gods or worship the image of gold you have set up.

Notice the boldness displayed by these three young men. Trust in God will give you boldness and confidence; it will give you the courage to look the enemy in the face and say, "Satan, I do not care what you do to me; I am not going to bow to you. You can throw me in the fire and turn up the heat, but I am not going to bow. You can deride my faith and mock my Christian confession, but I am not going to bow." Child of God, you do not have to allow fear and worry to control your life. You do not have to bow down in fear before the enemy; he is already defeated. Put your trust in God and watch Him do extraordinary things in your life.

Believers can cast our cares upon the Lord because He cares for us. God is concerned about His children, and He is intimately involved in our lives. God does not just care in the abstract; God cares about us specifically and personally. When God came to earth in the person of Jesus Christ, He most clearly demonstrated His deep concern for us. Jesus Christ can sympathize with our human weaknesses and struggles, or as the King James Version tells us in Hebrews 4:15, He can *"be touched with the feeling of our infirmities."* Jesus Christ can be touched with the feeling of your infirmities and the carefree life is a life lived in relationship with Him. Christ said in Matthew 11:28-30:

> *Come to Me, all you who labor and are heavy laden,*
> *and I will give you rest. Take My yoke upon you and*
> *learn from Me, for I am gentle and lowly in heart, and*
> *you will find rest for your souls. For My yoke is easy and*
> *My burden is light* (NKJV).

The yoke of Jesus does not lead to bondage and fear; it leads to freedom and rest.

Some of you may not be convinced that it is possible to cast your cares upon the Lord. "Dr. Graves, you just do not know what

I'm going through! I cannot pretend as if I do not have any problems! It does not matter what Peter said; I am just too realistic to be carefree." Peter, however, is not telling Christians to ignore the various troubles of life. He is not telling Christians to be naive or to live in a state of denial. When Peter tells us to cast our cares upon the Lord, he is not telling us to be careless. He is telling us to be carefree. We are to be carefree, not careless. There is a difference! First Peter 5:8 warns us quite clearly:

> *Be sober, be vigilant* [or watchful]; *because your adversary the devil walks about like a roaring lion, seeking whom he may devour* (NKJV).

Therefore, there are genuine evil forces about which to be concerned. Yet, we still are not to worry about them. We cannot and we must not allow the enemy to steal our joy. We cannot and we must not live in fear. We cannot and we must not give in to fear and worry. There are many reasons why it is sinful to worry. I will give you four.

One reason it is sinful to worry is that worry can become a form of idolatry, if we are not careful. Idolatry is not limited to the worship of statues. We commit the sin of idolatry when we allow anything or anyone other than God to capture our focus. Worry can become idolatry because, when we worry, we often magnify the problem rather than magnify God. We can be carefree only when our focus remains firmly fixed on the Living God. God is greater than terrorism, war, sickness and disease, gang violence, racism, and poverty. God is greater than all these things and since *"God is for us, who can be against us?"* (Rom. 8:31b).

Second, worry can sometimes lead to unbelief. Unbelief is a lack of belief or faith in God. The one who enters into unbelief becomes a skeptic and begins to contradict the very proclamations and the promises of God. Unbelief hinders our capacity to receive from God because we cannot receive from someone we do not fundamentally trust. Unbelief, then, is very destructive for the Christian.

Third, worry can be a form of pride, not humility. Worry is often an internal attempt to control events when in fact God already has everything under control. When we worry, we usually assume too much personal responsibility for the outcome of situations. This assumption is actually a form of pride. In First Peter 5:6, the apostle exhorts his readers to *"humble yourselves under the mighty hand of God, that He may exalt you in due time"* (NKJV). To cast our cares upon the Lord is to humble ourselves before Him. When we cast our cares upon the Lord, we do two things: (1) We acknowledge our complete dependence on God, and (2) We express our faith that He is fully able to handle our problems. Casting our cares upon the Lord is a sign of humility. I love it when the Bible describes God's hands as "mighty" hands in First Peter 5:6. Because God's hands are mighty, they are strong enough both to keep us secure and to handle any burdens that we cast upon Him.

Fourth and finally, worry does not change situations. Jesus asked in Matthew 6:27, *"Which of you by worrying can add one cubit to his stature?"* (NKJV). Most of the things we worry about are things that we cannot possibly change. Someone has said, "Worry is like a rocking chair. It will give you something to do, but it will not get you anywhere." Instead of worrying, we need to focus our attention on things that will build us up.

JOY IN JESUS CHRIST

A wonderful companion passage to First Peter 5:7 is Philippians 4:4-9. This latter passage encourages us to replace worry with worship, to pray, and to think about positive things. The apostle Paul exhorts the church in Philippians 4:4 to *"rejoice in the Lord always,"* to rejoice in the Lord under all circumstances. However, this is easier said than done. Countless problems plague us on a daily basis—financial problems, family problems, relationship problems, legal problems, health problems, and many other problems. How can we rejoice in the Lord when a loved one is dying from an incurable disease? How can we rejoice in the Lord in the midst of natural disasters like Hurricane Katrina or the earthquakes in Haiti or Chile? How can we rejoice in the Lord when divorce seems imminent? How can we rejoice in the Lord when global terrorism bombards us through our television screens? How can we rejoice in the Lord when the enemy opposes us at every turn? We experience so many trials and so many difficulties, yet the text clearly teaches us to rejoice in the Lord always.

I believe that a Christian should define "joy" differently than the world defines it. The world thinks of joy simply as an emotion. The joy conceived of by the world requires favorable circumstances. Webster's dictionary defines joy as *"the emotion evoked by well-being, success, or good fortune or by the prospect of possessing what one desires."*[4] However, the apostle Paul could encourage his readers to *"rejoice in the Lord always"* while he himself endured imprisonment, not too long before his execution. Moreover, in James 1:2-4, the apostle states emphatically:

> *My brethren, count it all joy when you fall into various trials, knowing that the testing of your faith produces patience. But let patience have its perfect work, that you may be perfect and complete, lacking nothing* (NKJV).

Clearly then, Christian joy is something that we can have even in the midst of trying circumstances.

Christian joy is not an emotion evoked by well-being and favorable circumstances; it is something much deeper than emotion. I did some research in the Greek language and found out that the words *joy* and *gladness* relate to the words *grace* and *gift*.[5] Thus, joy is a gift of God. Joy is one aspect of the grace of God that our

Lord wants liberally to supply to us. Scripture also tells us some other things about joy:

- Nehemiah 8:10 declares that the joy of the Lord is *our* strength.

- Psalm 16:11 (NKJV) states that fullness of joy is in God's presence.

- Psalm 43:4 proclaims that God Himself is the center and source of joy.

- Psalm 100 tells us that joy is one of the chief characteristics of worship.

I define joy as a gift from God, an aspect of His grace by which He manifests His presence to us, strengthens us, and enables us to serve Him with gladness regardless of the circumstances that we face. Therefore, joy is not the same thing as happiness. Happiness usually depends on what we are experiencing at the time, but we can experience Christian joy at all times. We can experience the joy of the Lord even when the circumstances of life are weighing us down.

We cannot *"rejoice in the Lord always"* without the Lord's help. To *"rejoice in the Lord always"* is not natural; it is supernatural. Only God can enable us to face financial difficulties, persecution, illnesses, tragedies, and other trials. Only God can provide the joy that we need in the midst of trying circumstances. True Christian joy comes through fellowshipping with God, through meditating on His Word, through drawing close to Him, through worship and prayer, and through casting our cares upon Him. Joy is a fruit of the Holy Spirit (see Gal. 5:22), so it belongs to all who believe in Christ.

To *"rejoice in the Lord always"* is to offer to the Lord a sacrifice of praise. Praise is a form of worship through which we magnify and glorify the Lord simply because He is God. Praise involves focusing on the greatness of God. Praise is different from thanksgiving, which involves gratitude to God for what He has done. We thank God for what He has done, but we praise God simply for who He is. Richard Foster describes the difference as follows:

> When I give thanks, my thoughts still circle about myself to some extent. But in praise my soul ascends to self-forgetting adoration, seeing and praising only the majesty and power of God, His grace and redemption.[6]

Praise is the perfect cure for self-centeredness. Sometimes we come into the presence of God demanding that He meet our needs immediately. Oftentimes, we conceive of prayer simply as a way of getting something *from* the Lord while forgetting about relationship *with* the Lord. Praise keeps us grounded. Praise reminds us that God created us to exalt and to glorify Him. As we begin to occupy our thoughts with the Lord's worthiness, self-centeredness grows weaker and weaker until we become satisfied with our Lord and with Him alone. As we praise God, the blessing of His presence overshadows any other blessing for which we could possibly hope.

Paul continues in Philippians 4:5, "*Let your gentleness be known to all men. The Lord is at hand*" (NKJV). We also could say, "Let your graciousness be known to all men...," or "Let your forbearance be known to all men...." Gentleness (graciousness or forbearance) is one of the attributes of Jesus Christ Himself. "Gentleness" prefers others above itself. One Bible scholar writes in his commentary, "Gentleness knows how to give way graciously and not insist on one's own rights."[7] Gentleness is the opposite of contention and self-seeking. It is one way of showing grace to others just as the Lord has shown grace to us. When we are in relationship with Christ, we will exhibit Christian behavior. The Christian can respond to others graciously because "*the Lord is at hand.*" This translation means that the Second Coming is imminent. We always should keep the Lord's Second Coming at the forefront of our thoughts.

Some Bibles have *"The Lord is near,"* rather than *"The Lord is at hand."* I personally like the translation, *"The Lord is near"* (NIV). This second translation implies that not only is the Lord coming back soon, but He is also near to us in locale.

- Jesus Christ is so near that He is knocking on the door of our hearts.

- He is so near that He can prevent us from stumbling on the road of life.

- He is so near that He can be touched with the feeling of our infirmities.

- He is so near that He can comfort us in the midst of a raging storm.

- He is so near that He is an ever-present help in times of trouble.

- He is so near that He sustains us with His mighty hand.

Because the Lord is near, His people should not fret or have anxiety about anything. Thus, Paul writes in Philippians 4:6, *"Be anxious for nothing, but in everything by prayer and supplication, with thanksgiving, let your requests be made known to God"* (NKJV). When Paul says, *"Be anxious for nothing,"* he is saying, "Do not worry!" Worry has no place in the life of a Christian because worry is evidence that a person lacks trust in the Lord. We should worry about nothing and pray about everything.

Oh what peace we often forfeit.
Oh what needless pains we bear.
All because we do not carry
Everything to God in prayer.

Are we weak and heavy laden,
Cumbered with a load of care?
Precious Savior still our refuge—
Take it to the Lord in prayer.[8]

Through prayer, Christians are to cast our cares upon the Lord. We must bring our worries to the altar and leave them there. Prayer is intimate communication between God and the believer. It is a dialogue. It requires listening on our part. Prayer is a way of drawing closer to God by sharing our most heartfelt requests with Him and allowing Him to minister back to us in the manner and in the timing that He chooses. God will speak to us through a still, small voice, gently impressing upon our minds His wisdom and His will. God will speak to us through the Bible. He will speak to us through other people, through an inspirational sermon, through a loving bit of encouragement from a friend, or through countless other creative ways. God will speak to us when we position ourselves to listen to Him. Paul says, *"In everything by prayer and supplication, with thanksgiving, let your requests be made known to God"* (Phil. 4:6 NKJV). Supplication is intense prayer. Instead of wasting our energy worrying about our problems, we need to spend that energy in prayer. We also need to make sure that as we petition the Lord to move on our behalf, we also thank Him for what He already has done in our lives. Thanksgiving reminds us that God has come through for us in the past; it also keeps us from being unduly concerned with our troubles; and it helps us to think about the needs of others who may be hurting even more than we are. Thanksgiving is closely related to praise. In both thanksgiving and praise, we give honor to the Lord. We get lost in God, and our problems begin to diminish in His presence.

Praise, prayer, and thanksgiving are powerful weapons against anxiety. If we take heed to Paul's encouragement, the result will be the peace of God. Paul says in verse 7, *"And the peace of God, which surpasses all understanding, will guard your hearts and minds through Christ Jesus"* (NKJV). The peace of God transcends human imagination. The peace of God is both the peace that God grants us and the tranquility in which He lives Himself.[9]

We can never experience the peace *of* God unless we have peace *with* God. We cannot expect the blessings of God until we are in relationship with God. If you do not know Jesus Christ as your Lord and Savior, then I challenge you to give your heart to Him today. Peace was one of the main themes of Jesus' ministry. He said:

> *Peace I leave with you, My peace I give to you; not as the world gives do I give to you. Let not your heart be troubled, neither let it be afraid* (John 14:27 NKJV).

Jesus Christ is our peace. He enables us to have peace with God and with one another. In fact, Isaiah describes Him as the *"Prince of Peace"* (Isa. 9:6). Peace in Scripture is a comprehensive term that includes the ideas of completeness, wholeness, fullness, well-being, and prosperity. In our text, the concept of peace suggests having a sense of tranquility, repose, or quiet rest. Christ is the embodiment and the source of supernatural peace. In fact, the Gospel of Jesus Christ is sometimes called the Gospel of peace. Ephesians 6, for example, refers to the Gospel of peace as one of the pieces of our spiritual armor. Therefore, the peace of God is a weapon against anxiety.

Paul concludes this passage in Philippians 4 with some practical advice. He says in verse 8:

> *Finally, brethren, whatever things **are** true, whatever things **are** noble, whatever things **are** just, whatever things **are** pure, whatever things **are** lovely, whatever things **are** of good report, if **there is** any virtue and if **there is** anything praiseworthy—meditate on these things* (NKJV).

Verse 7 speaks about the benefits of prayer. However, in addition to communicating with the Lord in prayer, Christians also need to fill their minds with the right things. If good food is necessary for physical health, then good thoughts are necessary for mental and spiritual health.[10]

Notice that Paul first encourages us to meditate on what is true. Jesus tells us in John 8:32 that the truth that we know makes us free. When we ponder, embrace, and repeat the things that we know to be true, the result is that God's truth becomes a part of us. We begin to adjust our thinking and actions to that which is right. The result is personal freedom. Paul also says to meditate on things that are noble, right, pure, lovely, and admirable.[11] Noble things are things that are worthy of honor and respect. Right things are things that are consistent with God's holiness and righteousness. Pure things are free from corruption. Lovely things are pleasing and attractive. Admirable things are the things that enjoy a solid reputation. Such things, according to Paul, are excellent and praiseworthy. They "are to be pondered and planned; the results will be beneficial for life and action."[12] Paul could have listed other things to meditate on, but his point is clear; we need to meditate on the things that glorify God and inspire us to emulate Jesus Christ.

In verse 9, Paul reminds his readers that he already has modeled the behavior that he is discussing. He says:

The things which you learned and received and heard and saw in me, these do, and the God of peace will be with you (NKJV).

Paul is a teacher who leads by example. He rejoices in the Lord while he suffers imprisonment; he fellowships with the Lord and experiences God's peace; he thinks on godly things and enjoys the Lord's tranquil presence. If we will obey the lessons of the apostle Paul, then we too can experience victory over worry and anxiety.

Child of God, the Lord loves you with an everlasting love. There is no good thing that He will withhold from you. Christ loves you so much that He gave His life for you. As your Great High Priest, He feels exactly what you feel. The Lord also sees your specific situation. He knows about the frustrating situation, the lost job, the family situation, the sickness, and the specific issues that need His attention. The Lord wants you to trust Him, to come to Him in faith, and to believe His Word. He hears you; He is with you; and He will never leave nor forsake you. Rejoice in the Lord despite the circumstances. Only then will you experience His peace, strength, and blessing. The Lord will deliver you. He will bring you out of bondage. He will meet you at your point of need. He will pour out His salvation into your life. He will make you whole.

Twelve Encouraging Scriptures

One of the most effective ways to combat worry, anxiety, and fear is to meditate on God's Word. Biblical meditation is the process of thinking about the Scriptures. The Hebrew word *hagah*, which is often translated "to meditate," literally means "to sigh, mutter, whisper, or ponder." Oftentimes, when we are trying to memorize something important, we will whisper it repeatedly to ourselves so that we will not forget it. This is what we should do with the Word of God. We should keep God's Word in our thoughts and on our lips. As Joshua 1:8 states:

Do not let this Book of the Law depart from your mouth; meditate on it day and night, so that you may be careful to do everything written in it. Then you will be prosperous and successful.

At this point in the book, you have probably encountered many Scriptures that have brought you great encouragement. I would like to provide 12 additional passages for you to ponder and memorize.

These verses will bless you tremendously. I also invite you to search the Bible for yourself and to receive its endless comfort. May you experience God's presence, peace, protection, and power as you meditate on His Word!

1. *The Lord is close to all who call on Him, yes, to all who call on Him in truth. He grants the desires of those who fear Him; He hears their cries for help and rescues them* (Ps. 145:18-19 NLT).

2. *You will keep in perfect peace all who trust in You, all whose thoughts are fixed on You* (Isa. 26:3 NLT).

3. *For You are my hiding place; You protect me from trouble. You surround me with songs of victory* (Ps. 32:7 NLT).

4. *I prayed to the Lord, and He answered me. He freed me from all my fears* (Ps. 34:4 NLT).

5. *For I am convinced that neither death nor life, neither angels nor demons, neither the present nor the future, nor any powers, neither height nor depth, nor anything else in all creation, will be able to separate us from the love of God that is in Christ Jesus our Lord* (Rom. 8:38-39).

6. *I am leaving you with a gift—peace of mind and heart. And the peace I give is a gift the world cannot give. So don't be troubled or afraid* (John 14:27 NLT).

7. *If you make the Lord your refuge, if you make the Most High your shelter, no evil will conquer you; no plague will come near your home* (Ps. 91:9-10 NLT).

8. *But the salvation of the righteous is from the Lord; He is their strength in the time of trouble. And the Lord shall help them and deliver them; He shall deliver them from the wicked, and save them, because they trust in Him* (Ps. 37:39-40 NKJV).

9. *Be sure of this: I am with you always, even to the end of the age* (Matt. 28:20b NLT).

10. *I have told you all this so that you may have peace in Me. Here on earth you will have many trials and sorrows. But take heart, because I have overcome the world* (John 16:33 NLT).

11. *When you lie down, you will not be afraid; yes, you will lie down and your sleep will be sweet. Do not be afraid of sudden terror, nor of trouble from the wicked when it comes; for the Lord will be your confidence, and will keep your foot from being caught* (Prov. 3:24-26 NKJV).

12. *Finally, be strong in the Lord and in His mighty power. Put on the full armor of God so that you can take your stand against the devil's schemes* (Eph. 6:10-11).

A Short Prayer to Cast Your Care Upon the Lord

Dear Heavenly Father, give me the strength to cast my care upon You, to hurl the things that weigh me down into Your loving and capable hands. Help me to know with confidence that You are with me and that You have everything under control. Free me, O God, from the cares and concerns of this life that prevent me from focusing my attention on You. Help me not to fret or to have any anxiety about anything. Give me a greater measure of Your joy and peace. Give me a greater awareness of Your presence. I love You, Lord, and I give You total control of my life. In the name of Jesus Christ, I pray. Amen.

Chapter Summary

1. God does not want us to live in a constant state of worry, fear, or emotional distress.

2. God desires for us to cast our cares upon Him (see 1 Pet. 5:7).

3. Casting our cares upon the Lord requires that we trust Him.

4. Worry can lead to idolatry, unbelief, and pride. It also fails to change our situations.

5. We need to replace worry with worship. We should rejoice in the Lord always, regardless of our circumstances (see Phil. 4:4-9).

6. Philippians 4:4-9 also encourages us to pray and to maintain an attitude of thanksgiving.

7. God will provide peace to those who seek Him.

8. One practical way believers can experience God's peace is to focus attention on positive things. Believers, as an act of the will, can choose to allow the goodness of God to dominate our thoughts.

Reflection/Discussion Questions

1. What new insights did you receive from reading this chapter?

2. How does freedom from worry relate to salvation and wholeness?

3. What types of things have you worried about in the past?

4. Why is it sinful to worry?

5. Define the term *joy*.

6. How can we rejoice in the Lord during difficult times?

7. Define the term *peace*.

8. What is the difference between "peace *with* God" and "the peace *of* God"?

9. Why does God deserve praise?

PRACTICAL APPLICATIONS AND ACTIVITIES

1. Write down ten things for which you are thankful.

2. Tell someone three things you will do to combat fear and worry in your life.

3. Pray with a friend or loved one about the troubling issues facing the two of you.

4. Tell someone this week about what you have learned about the peace of God.

CHAPTER 6

New Testament Provisions for Physical Healing

To justify the lack within his own heart of the fire of the Holy Spirit, the well-read theologian explains that the ancient way of knowing the things of God, taught and practiced by apostles and early Christians, is not for the present age.... Behold the folly of human reasoning! For as soon as this first power and illumination of the Spirit of God as a present work among men is denied for today, then nothing is left but the fleshly work and carnal wisdom of the old man. And the Church of Christ has become a kingdom of scribes and Pharisees.... And in none of the New Testament can a verse be found to show that Christ intended the gifts, workings and power of the Holy Spirit to diminish in the Church.

—William Law[1]

I believe that the ministry of healing is what moves the central doctrine of redemption and salvation from the realm of the abstract into the concrete reality of our lives.

—Francis MacNutt[2]

SPIRITUAL GIFTS

Ephesians 4:11 states:

It was He [i.e., Jesus Christ] *who gave some to be apostles, some to be prophets, some to be evangelists, and some to be pastors and teachers.*

The purpose of the ministries, according to verse 12, is *"to prepare God's people for works of service, so that the body of Christ may be built up."* God has given the Church a variety of spiritual gifts and special ministries so that His people will grow and become mature in the faith.

The topic of spiritual gifts is an exciting one. We read in the Bible about receiving direct messages from God, speaking in languages not previously learned, healing the sick, casting out demons, raising the dead, and performing extraordinary feats by the power of the Holy Spirit. Who can forget, for example, the restoration to health of the lame man at the gate called Beautiful in Acts 3 or the healing of a whole island of sick folk in Acts 28? God empowers ordinary men and women to accomplish His works of salvation. He gives spiritual gifts to the Body of Christ to meet all kinds of human needs.

Everyone has natural talents and abilities like cooking, singing, repairing automobiles, public speaking, mathematics, or playing baseball. Some of these talents and abilities are quite remarkable; however, they are not spiritual gifts. A spiritual gift is an ability that is specifically empowered by the Holy Spirit for use in the ministry of the Church.[3] Peter Wagner defines a spiritual gift as "a special attribute given by the Holy Spirit to every member of the Body of Christ, according to God's grace, for use within the context of the Body."[4] God gives spiritual gifts to equip the church to carry out its ministry until the Lord returns (see 1 Cor. 1:7).[5]

Every Christian has at least one spiritual gift (see 1 Pet. 4:10-11; 1 Cor. 12:7), but spiritual gifts may vary in strength, intensity, or scope (see Rom. 12:6; 1 Tim. 4:14; 2 Tim. 1:6). No matter what gifts may operate in someone's ministry, that person always should allow love to motivate his or her actions (see 1 Cor. 12:31–14:1).

There are three main discussions of spiritual gifts in the New Testament: Romans 12, First Corinthians 12, and Ephesians 4. We also may add First Corinthians 7:7, First Corinthians 13:3, and First Peter 4:9-10 to establish the following list of spiritual gifts: administration, apostle, celibacy, discerning of spirits, evangelist, exhortation, faith, giving, healing, helps, hospitality, knowledge, leadership, mercy, martyrdom, miracles, pastor, prophecy, service, teaching, tongues and interpretation of tongues, voluntary poverty, and wisdom. There probably are many other spiritual gifts.[6] There may be as many spiritual gifts as there are needs in the community. The Holy Spirit distributes gifts to meet the numerous challenges that we face.

With any spiritual gift, one or more of the following happens: (1) God reveals something to our minds; (2) God empowers our speech; or (3) God enables us to do some action.[7] Effective operation in spiritual gifts requires connection to the mind, heart, and power of God. We should avoid the things that displease God and yield ourselves to His control. We can think of the use of spiritual gifts as participation with God. God actually does the work of revealing, healing, mending, or restoring, but He allows us to work with Him to address some human need. Therefore, if we are to work with God, we need to know something about how God operates. What are God's priorities? How does God view the situation about which we are praying? What does God's Word tell us about the issue that we are facing? The bottom line is this—spiritual gifts are not mysterious; they are the ways that God equips His people to meet the various tasks of ministry. They are the ways that He has chosen to meet our needs. Although God does not need us in an absolute sense, He has chosen us as His agents of blessing in the world.

As we observe those around us, we must admit that it seems that some people have received special grace from God to do certain activities better than most others. Some people preach with unique authority and power. Others can make the most difficult truths accessible to just about anyone. Still others are effective organizers, administrators, leaders, or encouragers. God also enables some of His children to do many of the more remarkable things that we see in the Bible. God often uses me to bring physical healing to the sick and comfort to the suffering.

God has not given us all the same gifts and abilities, and it is a beautiful thing when we all work together as one body to accomplish His will. My prayer is that you will discover your spiritual gifts and that you will develop these gifts for the glory of God and the benefit of the Church. Some spiritual gifts, such as teaching and administration, may be permanent possessions. Other gifts, such as those in First Corinthians 12:8-10, may be available to all Christians when the occasion requires their manifestation. As we discover who God has created us to be, let us also open ourselves up to ways in which He may wish to stretch us beyond our present comfort zones.

The cultivation of spiritual gifts requires trial and error in Christian environments. You should practice the use of gifts in loving and supportive atmospheres, such as small group settings, Bible studies, or intercessory prayer meetings. Start praying for the sick. Teach a Sunday school class. Share with others what you think God is revealing to you. Spiritual gifts emerge as we extend ourselves lovingly to meet various needs within the Body of Christ.

As you stretch out in faith, do so in a spirit of humility. Do not be afraid to receive instruction or correction from leaders. Do not be afraid to receive guidance from those with proven gifts in a certain area. It is a good idea to acquire and spend time with a mentor. Watch, shadow, and serve the mentor. The only way to get proficient at anything in the natural or spiritual realms is to practice. Through the years, I have greatly benefitted from the wisdom and guidance of Sunday school teachers, pastors, denominational leaders, engineers, scientists, professors, writers, businesspeople, and a host of others whom God brought into my life at significant times. I now have the privilege of mentoring a number of individuals myself in both educational and spiritual matters.

Once a particular gift does emerge, the community will recognize it. The gift itself will produce results. Make sure that the leadership within a particular fellowship acknowledges your gift before you begin to operate independently. If God calls you to a specific ministry, you will have the inward testimony of the Holy Spirit that compels you to go forth in that ministry. Like Jeremiah, the Word will be like fire *"shut up in* [your] *bones"* (Jer. 20:9). The Lord also will equip you with the gifts for the task of ministry. The testimony both of leadership and the laity of the church will confirm that God has called you to the ministry and the fruit of your ministry will attest to the call.

In order to operate effectively in spiritual gifts, we must submit ourselves to the will of God. First Corinthians 12:11 (NKJV) tells us that the Holy Spirit distributes the gifts as He wills. We discern the will of God through daily prayerful meditation on the Word of God, through hearing the preached Word, through receiving wise counsel, through submitting to leadership, and through quieting ourselves before the Lord in order to allow Him to put thoughts into our minds.

In order to operate effectively in spiritual gifts, we must desire for God to receive glory as His Kingdom advances on earth. Some people want spiritual gifts as badges of honor to increase their status in the Church; however, spiritual gifts are not for human glory—they are for the glory of God. God receives glory as He meets human needs. If we truly wish to develop spiritually, then we must forsake pride and focus ourselves on glorifying the Heavenly Father.

To operate in spiritual gifts, we need to pursue the heart of God. God is good, compassionate, merciful, and generous. The love of God is the real power behind spiritual gifts. This is why First Corinthians 13 (a chapter on love) lies between First Corinthians 12 and First Corinthians 14 (two chapters on spiritual gifts). As we help other people, pray for them, and do what we can to bless them, spiritual gifts will emerge.

Recently, my good friend Sonja Sharp and I prayed for a woman who was exhibiting symptoms of multiple sclerosis. As we petitioned the Lord for healing, I did not sense any physical manifestations of power—only a deep sense of compassion for this young woman of barely 20. As we lovingly ministered to her, the symptoms soon disappeared and have not returned in nearly a year.

Spiritual gifts such as healing may come as we reflect on the Word of God. Many times, a truth in God's Word will "jump off the page" and bring the answer that we need. Forgiveness also aids in the effectiveness of spiritual gifts such as healing. Unforgiveness is a hindrance to the operation of spiritual gifts and to answered prayer (see Matt. 6:14-15; Mark 11:22-26). In order for God to release healing into our lives, we must forgive others. Forgiveness is a choice. Is there someone in your life you need to forgive? Consider the following simple prayer: "Father, I was really hurt by _____, but I choose to forgive _____ just as You have forgiven me. Please heal the negative memories that are affecting me and draw _____ closer to You. In the name of Jesus Christ, I pray. Amen." Allow God to minister to you now by His Spirit. If you have offended someone from whom you need to seek forgiveness, it would be wise to clear the air just as soon as possible.

Expectation, desire, and persistence can increase the manifestation of spiritual gifts (see 1 Cor. 12:31). Most individuals who came to Jesus for miracles expected to receive from Him (see Mark 5:25-34; Mark 7:24-30). We too can come before God with boldness and confidence (see Heb. 4:14-16).

Worship prepares our hearts to receive from God. When we worship God, we magnify Him above our problems. Whether we are singing to the Lord by ourselves at home or praising Him in a corporate setting, we can receive a strengthening of faith through worship. Worship enables us to shift our focus from our problems to the Living God.

Finally, the continual infilling of the Holy Spirit stirs up spiritual gifts (see Acts 4:23-31). I have found, for example, that praying in tongues intensifies other gifts such as healing. The Holy Spirit is our Helper and the distributor of gifts. The more we yield to Him, the more effective we become in life and ministry.

INSIGHTS ON PHYSICAL HEALING FROM THE BOOK OF JAMES

James 5:14-16 is the only passage in the letters of the New Testament that specifically focuses on the issue of physical healing.[8] James instructs the sick to call for the elders of the church. Church leaders often have the wisdom and maturity to help the afflicted to deal with sickness. They also may possess certain spiritual gifts, such as healing, or will know how to mobilize others with these gifts to serve those in need.

When the elders arrive, they pray over the sick person and anoint the person with oil. Prayer is a provision from God for all who are suffering (see James 5:13). The oil reminds the suffering person of the Lord's presence. Although people used oil in the ancient world as a medicine, the oil spoken about here probably is symbolic of the Holy Spirit (see Acts 10:38 cf. Luke 3:22; Luke 4:18-19 cf. Isa. 61:1ff.). The elders anoint the sick person *"in the name of the Lord."* Therefore, Jesus Christ Himself is the authority and the source of power behind the act. The Lord Jesus Christ is a healer. When He died on the cross, He paid the redemptive price not only for our sins, but also for the effects of sin. Whenever God heals a person, He demonstrates the victory of His Son over sin and sickness. Christ:

> *Was wounded for our transgressions; He was bruised for our iniquities; the chastisement of our peace was upon Him, and by His stripes, we are healed* [healing has come to us] (Isaiah 53:5 NKJV).

Notice that James does not instruct the sick person to pray, but to call for the elders of the church. The sick person may be too weak to pray. He or she will need the intercession of others. Intercession is a powerful form of prayer that fosters interdependence in the Body of Christ.

The first part of James 5:15 indicates that the prayer offered in faith will make the sick person well. The Greek literally says that the prayer of faith will "save" the sick or make the sick person "whole." The Lord Jesus Christ is the object of faith. Faith is not just the belief that the Lord will heal; faith is the belief in the Lord Himself. The text assures us that the Lord will minister lovingly to the one in need and raise the person up. Even if the person is on medication, which is certainly advisable, the actual healing will come from the Lord. The Lord, not the prayer, the faith, or the power of the elders raises the sick person up. Christ will do for the sick person what is ultimately best for him or her from God's perspective.

If sin happens to be the cause of the illness, confession of the sin brings restoration and healing. Heartfelt confession of sin requires humility, and God promises to give grace to the humble (see James

4:6). From a natural perspective, confession of sin can lead to the release of stress, guilt, and other emotional bondage that can promote illness. James 5:15b does not imply, though, that the cause of all sickness is the sin of the one who is sick (e.g., see John 9:1-3). Although James instructs his readers to call for the elders when sick, he indicates that not only elders have effective prayers. The prayers of all God's people effect change when hindrances such as sin, unbelief, and pride are removed (see also 2 Chron. 7:14). Why are prayers so effective? 1) Prayers are effective because God allows us to participate with Him in accomplishing His plans on earth and 2) Prayers are effective because God Himself answers prayer. God is all-powerful, and He chooses to respond to the humble requests of His people.

Why Some People Do Not Receive Physical Healing Immediately

Not everyone for whom we pray receives physical healing immediately. As is true of all prayer, prayers for healing must coincide with God's will and timing (see 1 John 5:14-15). In rare cases, the infirmity of the individual for whom we pray may be redemptive (see Gal. 4:13-14). If God does not choose to heal a person physically, then His decision is not uncaring or indiscriminate. If the *only* factor preventing physical healing is God's will and other factors, such as sin, unbelief, or demonic causes, are not involved, then we can take comfort in the fact that God's decision not to heal a person physically is the best possible choice for the person with the best possible ultimate outcome. Hence, in God's divine perspective, the person is better off without the healing. Yet, redemptive purposes for sickness are the exception and not the rule. The normative pattern for Christian healing is James 5:14-16. Never assume that it is not God's will to heal unless God explicitly communicates this to you. Sickness and death are enemies resulting from the Fall of humanity that will ultimately be destroyed (see Rev. 21:4).

Closely related to God's will is His timing. Some healings are immediate. Others are gradual. Some occur after a period of consistent prayer. Some do not occur in this life.[9] We cannot tell God how or when to answer a prayer. We must pray in confidence and then leave the results to the Heavenly Father. If prayer does not lead to immediate healing, then it certainly will lead to wisdom regarding God's pathway to healing or to insights regarding other concerns that God desires to address first. Never think that your prayers are unheard or ineffective!

Faith is also an essential component of prayer. Jesus affirms the importance of faith in Matthew 7:7-11, Mark 11:22-24, Luke 11:9-13, and John 15:7. James also stresses the need for faith in prayer in 1:5-8. If doubt is present in our hearts, this can be a hindrance to our prayers. In addition, if we pray for things that are outside the will of God, then we do not pray in faith. The key to faith is its object, Jesus Christ, not the things for which we pray.

Sometimes what hinders a person from receiving physical healing is that he or she has failed to discover God's ordained method for healing. For example, a person may be praying individually for healing, and God may have ordained for someone else to offer a prayer that will effect healing. God may also choose to bring healing through natural means, such as medicine, diet, exercise, or surgery.[10] We should seek God for wisdom in order to discover our individual pathway to physical healing (see James 1:5).

Sometimes sin is the cause of sickness (see 1 Cor. 11:29-30). We cannot be selective in our obedience to God and then expect God's hand in our lives. Many individuals have received physical healing after a time of repentance or after forgiveness of a brother or sister in Christ. Jesus connects forgiveness to answered prayer in Mark 11:22-25. Not all sickness is the result of sin or lack of faith, though (see John 9:1-3); some sicknesses have demonic causes (see Mark 9:25) or other undiscovered causes. In all cases of sickness, we should seek God for wisdom. Receiving God's wisdom and perspective in prayer prevents us from misdiagnosis (e.g., praying for emotional healing when there is a demonic cause or vice versa) and helps us to pray specifically. Effective prayer requires diligence on our part.

SEVERAL EXAMPLES OF PHYSICAL HEALING

Physical healing should be a normative part of the ministry of the Church. God will manifest His healing power in our personal lives and through our prayers for others as we petition Him to do so. Below are a few of the many cases of physical healing I have seen through the years.

My earliest memory of physical healing is from childhood. My father and a few other elders of the church prayed for a man in a wheelchair. I do not know the condition from which he suffered. The prayers of the elders evidently resulted in a cure, and the man began to walk. I never forgot that demonstration of the love and power of God. The incident revealed to me that God actually does answer prayers for healing.

God can even heal animals if it suits His purposes.[11] When I was younger, I had a puppy named Princess. One day, as I was riding my bicycle, Princess jetted in front of me, and I ran over her leg and neck. She was in tremendous pain! I was initially very upset, but I remembered that the elders of the church often placed oil on the sick when they prayed for them, so I went into the house to get some olive oil. I anointed Princess and prayed for her (for a dog!). At that moment, she got up and jumped around playfully. She stopped limping and was in no obvious pain, as she had been in just minutes earlier. I was no theologian or Bible scholar at the time, but I knew that God was a healer. His condescension to my simple request developed within me a confidence to bring my petitions before Him.

Often during my childhood, I would pray for people suffering with various minor ailments. In fifth grade, for example, I prayed on separate occasions for a teacher and a fellow classmate who were bothered by headaches. The headaches left immediately, to the surprise of them both. Around that time, I also prayed for my grandmother who had a headache and other pain. I read a Bible verse to her and prayed; the pain left immediately. She told me afterward that she could feel the tangible healing power of the Holy Spirit as I laid hands on her.

Years later, I would experience a tangible manifestation of healing power myself. I was a sophomore in college and suffering pain in my neck and shoulders. While praising the Lord in a morning time of devotion, I could feel the tangible healing power of the Holy Spirit as a heat flowing through the painful areas. The pain left immediately.

The Lord often manifests His healing power in tangible ways. About 11 years ago, I prayed for a man named Hank. He expressed to me that he was battling several addictions, including one to gambling and another to cigarettes. He also told me that he sensed a large gulf between God and himself. The Lord's power came on him and he fell to the floor. He told me that he felt God's peace and exclaimed, "I have never in my life felt this close to God." I gave Hank a few Scriptures to ponder before moving on to pray for others. I had the privilege of speaking with Hank some time later. He no longer suffered with the addictions.

It is amazing how God will use ordinary people to accomplish His will and purposes. Each new day provides tremendous opportunities to present ourselves to God for His use. One day, I left work early in order to pick up some items at home before heading to a theology class. When I arrived at home, I suddenly became troubled and did not know the source of my agitation. I decided to go outside for a moment to clear my thoughts. As I stood outside,

I encountered a man in his early 20s and I discerned that he was going through a spiritual trial. I asked him what was happening in his life and he expressed to me that he was a new Christian and suffered some lingering effects of addiction to alcohol. I prayed for him and he fell to the ground quite unexpectedly, under the power of God. He experienced deliverance from his addiction and visible peace. I do not know what eventually became of him, but I do know that God met him in a special way on that occasion.

In my journal entry for February 6, 1997, I wrote of the healing of a classmate of mine in seminary who had a degenerative condition in her hip and walked with a cane. As I prayed for her in the library chapel, she expressed to me that she could sense the Lord's presence. Healing occurred immediately, and she was able to move around without pain. She could cross her legs, dance, and walk briskly without the assistance of her cane. Several weeks later, she was still pain-free, and the healing became a glorious testimony to her family members and friends.

Several days later, I recorded in my journal the healing of a woman named Jill. Several friends and I prayed for Jill on Saturday, February 15, 1997. Her left arm was in a sling and had been afflicted for several years. After we prayed for her, Jill received an instantaneous healing and removed her arm from the sling. The next day in church, she gave a testimony of how God had healed her arm. She also informed the congregation that she was deaf in her left ear prior to receiving prayer the day before. God restored her hearing during the night, the news of which caused considerable excitement and amazement among the people.

It always thrills me to see how God lovingly ministers to hurting people. I witness quite frequently the manifestation of His grace in physical healing of the sick. Few things cause as much joy as witnessing the reversal of paralysis, the breaking of addictions, the restoration of vision, or the remission of cancer. Three dear women approached me recently with healing testimonies. One had suffered for weeks with a bleeding condition. Another had a tumor on her ovaries. Both experienced release from these afflictions in a church service in which I ministered to the sick. The third woman was partially deaf in her right ear. As I prayed for her, she felt "hot oil" flow through her ear and her hearing improved. Not every healing is immediate or dramatic; however, God will use us to bring wholeness to hurting people if we will only present ourselves to Him for His use.

A Personal Testimony of Physical Healing

I myself am a grateful recipient of God's healing touch. In the latter half of June 2001, I began to experience a number of health-related problems, including frequent urination and fatigue. These problems came upon me suddenly, literally overnight. Over the next few weeks, the problems persisted and I experienced severe dehydration and blurry vision. At times, my eyes felt as if they had no moisture in them. One day, my eyesight was so poor that I could not read with or without my glasses. After I did a little research, I discovered that these problems were symptoms of diabetes. On Friday, July 13, I scheduled an appointment with my doctor to have a complete physical. The time for the appointment was set for Monday, July 30.

In my research of diabetes, I discovered that the type 2 variety of the disease often responded to proper diet and exercise. Armed with this knowledge, I took several steps to eliminate all excess sugar and carbohydrates from my diet. I also made sure to get regular exercise. Within about a week or so of scheduling my doctor's appointment, I noticed that most of the serious diabetic symptoms had disappeared. This in itself was a major victory for me because I no longer felt powerless against the advancement of an incurable disease.

Throughout my battle with the diabetic symptoms, my Christian friends were a vital source of encouragement to me. One friend told me to have faith and to trust in God. She said, "I know that God is going to give you a good report." Another friend told me to believe God for a miracle of healing because I had much work to do for the Kingdom of God. Others encouraged me through prayer and through helpful advice. Everyone with whom I shared my ordeal, both charismatic and non-charismatic, seemed confident that God would extend His healing grace to me and bring me out of the trial victoriously. The love and concern that I felt from the people of God made me appreciate the Lord's community of believers even more than I had previously.

My parents also were tremendous sources of strength. They encouraged me through the Scriptures and reminded me of the love of God and His absolute authority over the created order. My mom expressed that she believed that God would perform a miracle for me, and my dad reminded me that the same Lord who healed the sick and delivered the oppressed in the Bible was the Lord whom I served.

From the very beginning of my physical challenge, I believed that if I could discover the will of God in the midst of the situation, then I would win the battle against diabetes (see 1 John 5:14-15). Even if I experienced a delay in the reception of physical healing, I knew that God only wills what is best for me. Therefore, I could rest in His love, sovereignty, and character as I waited for an answer to my prayers.

As I sought the Lord for a physical cure, I thought about His gracious answers to my prayers for others. He had blessed many people through my ministry. Now I needed His help! During the week of July 22, 2001, I asked God for greater clarity of His will and purposes. His answer was Hebrews 11:6b: *"He is a rewarder of those who diligently seek Him"* (NKJV). I also began pondering the story of the woman with the issue (flow) of blood (see Matt. 9:20-22; Mark 5:25-34; Luke 8:43-48). I was encouraged by the woman's boldness and expectation, and I figured that if Jesus could heal her issue (flow) of blood, then He could heal my issue (problem) of blood.

With each passing moment, I became more convinced that it was God's will to heal me. In fact, God seemed to urge me to take authority over the disease that was attacking my body. Therefore, I began to pray with more hope and greater expectation, and I began to take more of an aggressive stance against anything happening in my life that opposed God's will. God gave me a firm confidence that He would apply the reality of Isaiah 53:5 and First Peter 2:24 to my physical state just as He had applied it to my spiritual state. In other words, God would use my trial to demonstrate to me that every good gift that He gives comes from the terrible (and wonderful) price that Jesus Christ paid at Calvary (see also Matt. 8:16-17). Although I was still in the midst of the trial, I began to experience the grace and mercy of God to an overwhelming degree. As Mary responded to the angel Gabriel, I could only say, *"Let it be to me according to your word"* (Luke 1:38 NKJV).

On Friday, July 27, a friend of mine received distressing news. His mother received a diagnosis of breast cancer. I visited with him on Saturday, July 28, and we had a powerful time of prayer for her. After we had prayed for about an hour, I asked him to pray briefly for me concerning the meeting with my doctor that was to occur on Monday, July 30. He asked God to strengthen me and to restore my health, and he encouraged me prophetically not to accept any negative reports before God had completed His process of healing.

On Monday, July 30, I went to my doctor's appointment. I was feeling quite well physically, much better than I had felt previously. The blurry vision that I had experienced earlier in the month had ceased by this point. I underwent a complete physical and had blood drawn for the diabetes testing. I also discussed several dietary issues with my doctor.

Early Tuesday morning at around 4:00 or 5:00 in the morning, I had a prophetic dream (or vision). In the first scene, I was ministering to the sick. I laid my hands on some people; over others, I simply spoke a word. There was a tremendous atmosphere for healing and deliverance, and most, if not all, received what they were expecting from God. After interceding for others, I laid hands on myself and asked the Lord to heal and to bless me. In the second part of the dream while I was on a beach, the Lord indicated that He would heal me. I asked if He would do it within seven days, and He responded that He would do it in five days. This meant that if I took the timing of the dream literally, the Lord would heal me on Sunday, August 5, 2001.

On Saturday, August 4, I received a negative report. The results of the previous Monday's physical arrived in the mail. Everything was okay except for my blood sugar level. My sugar level was 139 mg/dL. Diabetes is defined as a sugar level greater than 125 mg/dL when a person has fasted overnight. If someone's blood sugar level is greater than 125 mg/dL on two consecutive medical visits, then that person is diagnosed with the disease.

I cannot honestly say that I was totally without fear and concern on Saturday, August 4, but I can say that God sustained me with His strength and His presence. Faith is not a denial of circumstances; it is an unwavering trust in God that looks beyond circumstances to the one who is the source of all life and wholeness. I have discovered that God often will honor the relationship that I have with Him even when I fail to remain strong emotionally. God is there with me during my mountaintop experiences, and He is there with me in the valleys as well.

On Sunday, August 5, I went to church. It was communion Sunday. Before the service, I approached one of the "church mothers," Nettie Cole, and told her that I had been battling high blood sugar. The church mother, who was age 80 at the time and who regularly intercedes for me and for my ministry, immediately responded, "The devil is a liar. Mother wants you to take care of yourself. Make sure you eat right, but God is going to heal you right now." She then prayed for me and commanded my blood sugar level to return to normal according to the will of the Lord. I believed that God would honor His word that I received in the dream five days earlier. I later partook of the communion elements with the grateful awareness of the healing and salvation provided by the broken body and shed blood of the Savior.

On the evening of August 5, I had the privilege of praying on the phone with my friend's mother who had received the diagnosis of breast cancer. It was a four-way conference-style prayer meeting, with my friend and me praying in Pasadena, California, and his mother and sister praying in Atlanta, Georgia. I believed that it was God's will to heal the breast cancer, so I prayed along those lines. I was very much encouraged by her strong faith and love for the Lord.

On Wednesday, August 8, I went to have my blood sugar retested. My parents and a close friend prayed with me that morning that God would allow me to receive a good report. I asked the Lord that since He had promised to heal me that He would allow my blood sugar level to be in the middle of the normal range. Since normal blood sugar ranges from 70-110 mg/dL, I asked the Lord to give me a result of (70 + 110)/2 or 90 mg/dL.

On Friday, August 17, the results of my second test arrived in the mail. I quickly opened the letter to read the good news. My blood sugar measured 89 mg/dL, one point lower than I had expected! A few minutes later, I checked my e-mail messages and read a message from my friend whose mother had received the diagnosis of cancer. His mother now showed no signs of cancer, to the utter amazement of her doctors. The words of Psalm 107:20 took on new meaning that day (see also Matt. 8:8).

I pray that Christians reading this account will be reminded that God is greater than all human challenges. He is an ever-present help in all circumstances. I also pray that non-Christians reading this account will give their hearts to Jesus Christ, making Him Lord and accepting Him as Savior. The same Lord who heals the physical body can save the sin-sick soul.

A PRAYER FOR PHYSICAL HEALING

Heavenly Father, I thank You for this precious time to worship You, meditate on Your Word, and petition You for physical healing. I ask the Holy Spirit to empower this time of prayer so that I will be in Your perfect will. Forgive my sins, dear God, and create within me a clean heart. Let everything that I think, say, do, and experience bring glory and honor to You. Father, I praise You for Your Word and for the power that it contains. Studying the Scriptures is the most reliable way for me to come into alignment with Your perfect will. So now, with reverence and humility, I declare some of the things that Your Word says about healing.

Read Scriptures concerning healing, health, life, faith, answered prayer, and God's faithfulness. A few suggestions include the following: Third John 2; Jeremiah 17:14; James 5:14-15; John 10:10; Luke 10:19; Isaiah 41:10; Psalm 30:2; 107:19-20; Matthew 7:7-8; First John 5:14-15; John 15:7; Isaiah 55:11; Jeremiah 1:12; Joshua 21:45; Psalm 91:16; 118:17; Mark 11:22-23; Matthew 4:23-25; and Luke 4:40. At some point, you should read all these verses in context.

Dear Father, I believe what Your Word says concerning healing and answered prayer. Therefore, I ask You in faith to heal me. Destroy the hold that sickness has on my body. Deliver me from diabetes, fatigue, imbalances [be specific with your physical needs], *and other problems. Please give me a fresh start in the name of Your Son, Jesus Christ.*

I now command my body to recover and to receive the healing and wholeness that God extends to me right now. I speak to every cell, tissue, organ, and system in my body, and command these to come into alignment with the perfect will of God. Be made whole in the name of the Lord. Be restored in the name of the Lord. By the stripes of Jesus Christ, I receive healing. Holy Spirit, please apply to me the full benefit of the person and work of Jesus Christ so that I will receive wholeness. Every provision for healing I need is in Christ. I now stir up the gifts of the Holy Spirit. I stir up the gift of faith, gifts of healings, and gifts of miracles. I invite You, dear God, to manifest Your power to accomplish whatever You will to accomplish.

Place your hands on your forehead or over the area of your body that needs healing. If you have received the gift of tongues, pray gently in the Spirit for a few minutes. If you have not received the gift of tongues, then wait silently in God's presence. Some of you will feel a tangible sense of God's presence, like a feeling of warmth or a gentle current, but others of you may not feel anything. God can heal you with or without feelings.

Father, thank You for what You have done and what You are doing in my body. I receive everything that You have for me and I give You all glory, honor, and praise. In the name of the Lord Jesus Christ, I pray. Amen.

Chapter Summary

1. God gives spiritual gifts to equip the Body of Christ for service.

2. When Christians learn to operate in spiritual gifts, the Body of Christ receives strength and becomes more effective.

3. We discover and develop spiritual gifts in a loving Christian atmosphere.

4. God can heal us through gifts of healings and offers a pattern for healing ministry in James 5:14-16.

5. We should seek God for wisdom in every challenge that we face so that we may uncover His pathway for our healing.

6. My personal case of healing followed the brief timeline below:

   - June 2001—I noticed symptoms of diabetes.

   - July 13, 2001—I scheduled a doctor's appointment for July 30, 2001.

   - July 27, 2001—A friend's mother received a diagnosis of breast cancer.

   - July 28, 2001—My friend and I prayed concerning his mother. He encouraged me not to accept any negative reports before God completed His work of healing in my life.

   - July 30, 2001—I had a complete physical and was tested for diabetes.

   - July 31, 2001—God gave me a dream (vision) in which He told me that He would heal me in five days. I asked God to give me a blood sugar level of 90, which lies midway between the lower (70) and upper (110) levels of normal blood sugar.

- August 4, 2001—Four days after the dream, I received the report from my first physical. It indicated a fasting blood sugar level of 139. Diabetes is diagnosed when two fasting blood sugar tests give results above 125.

- August 5, 2001—This was the fifth day after the dream, the day that I understood that God would heal me. I received prayer from one of my intercessors. She said that God would heal me that moment. She did not know about my dream. Later, my friend, his mother, his sister, and I prayed on the phone concerning the cancer diagnosis.

- August 8, 2001—I had the second blood test administered.

- August 17, 2001—I received the results from my second blood test. My blood test measured 89, one point lower than I had asked. I also received word by e-mail that my friend's mother was cancer-free.

Reflection/Discussion Questions

1. What new insights did you receive from reading this chapter?

2. Do you need physical healing in your life? Does the present chapter give you any hope?

3. What is a spiritual gift?

4. Why are elders important to the healing process?

5. Why is repentance of sins important to the healing process?

6. Why is wisdom important when we face sicknesses, trials, and hardships?

Practical Applications and Activities

1. Write down several Scriptures related to physical healing other than the ones included in this chapter.

2. Testify to a friend about any physical healing that you received during your prayer time.

3. Discuss your physical situation with a medical doctor. Does he or she suggest any course of action for your physical health? If you received physical healing through prayer, what does your doctor say about the new status of your health?

CHAPTER 7

When Only a Miracle Will Do

It is not enough merely to say, "I am a Christian," and then in practice to live as if present contact with the supernatural were something far off and strange. Many Christians I know seem to act as though they come in contact with the supernatural just twice—once when they are justified and become a Christian and once when they die. The rest of the time they act as though they were sitting in the materialist's chair.

—Francis Schaeffer[1]

People in our culture need to see that God is more powerful than the lifestyles they are serving. We are discovering that scripturally defined signs and wonders are playing a major role in getting the Gospel message out to a nation that needs help and spiritual direction.

—John Wimber[2]

AN ATMOSPHERE FOR MIRACLES

The third and fourth chapters of the Book of Acts recount the dramatic healing of a lame man and the powerful effect that the miracle has on the people who see it. Let us consider a few selected verses from this story.

Now Peter and John went up together to the temple at the hour of prayer, the ninth hour. And a certain man lame from his mother's womb was carried, whom they laid daily at the gate of the temple which is called Beautiful, to ask alms from those who entered the temple; who, seeing Peter and John about to go into the temple, asked for alms. And fixing his eyes on him, with John, Peter said, "Look at us." So he gave them his attention, expecting to receive something from them. Then Peter said, "Silver and gold I do not have, but what I do have I give you: In the name of Jesus Christ of Nazareth, rise up and walk." And he took him by the right hand and lifted him up, and immediately his feet and ankle bones received strength. So he, leaping up, stood and walked and entered the temple with them—walking, leaping, and praising God. And all the people saw him walking and praising God. Then they knew that it was he who sat begging alms at the Beautiful Gate of the temple; and they were filled with wonder and amazement at what had happened to him (Acts 3:1-10).[3]

By the time we reach Acts 4:16, Peter and John have been preaching the Gospel, and thousands of people have come to faith in Jesus Christ. The religious authorities are extremely angry, and Peter and John are arrested. Yet, no one can deny that a genuine miracle has taken place. In Acts 4:16-17, some of the religious officials ask, *"What shall we do to these men?"* and then they remark:

For, indeed, that a notable miracle has been done through them is evident to all who dwell in Jerusalem, and we cannot deny it. But so that it spreads no further among the people, let us severely threaten them, that from now on they speak to no man in this name.

Verse 18 says that the council of religious leaders *"commanded* [Peter and John] *not to speak at all nor teach in the name of Jesus."* However, the apostles disregard the threats of the religious council. The leaders of the council eventually release Peter and John from prison for lack of evidence, and the apostles commit themselves to preach the Gospel of Jesus Christ with even greater intensity than before.

In Acts 4:24-31, the church prays intensely for a move of God. Verses 29-31 read as follows:

> *"Now, Lord, look on their threats, and grant to Your servants that with all boldness they may speak Your word, by stretching out Your hand to heal, and that signs and wonders may be done through the name of Your holy Servant Jesus." And when they had prayed, the place where they were assembled together was shaken; and they were all filled with the Holy Spirit, and they spoke the word of God with boldness.*

Concluding with verse 33, *"And with great power the apostles gave witness to the resurrection of the Lord Jesus. And great grace was upon them all."*

I have entitled this section, "An Atmosphere for Miracles." A miracle is an unusual manifestation of God's power with which He glorifies Himself and causes wonder and amazement among people. Acts 3 and 4 reveal an atmosphere in which God brings physical healing, joy, salvation, spiritual vitality, and holy boldness. It is an atmosphere of preaching and prayer, faith and expectancy, and remarkable spiritual power. It is an atmosphere for miracles.

I am sure that many readers of this book are asking God for miracles. Many of you are hurting tremendously. Some of you, like the man in this text, need physical healing. Others of you are praying for financial breakthroughs. Still others of you are suffering from emotional distress, relational conflicts, fear, confusion, or harassment from the enemy. I am no different from you. Several areas in my personal life need a manifestation of God's love, grace, and power. The good news for all of us is that God still works miracles today.

The Bible is a book of miracles. In Exodus, God rescues the children of Israel from captivity. He judges Egypt by sending ten plagues, and He splits the Red Sea in two so that His people can cross on dry ground. Psalm 77:14 celebrates God's miraculous deliverance of His people. It reads, *"You are the God who does wonders; You have declared Your strength among the peoples."* In First and Second Kings, the prophets Elijah and Elisha experience miracles in their ministries. Elijah, for example, prays and a widow's son rises from the dead. In Elisha's ministry, a Shunammite woman also has her son restored to life.

In the earthly ministry of Jesus Christ, humanity experienced God's miracle-working power at an unprecedented level. Jesus restored sight to the blind; He opened deaf ears; He gave mobility to the crippled; and He cast out evil spirits. The Lord fed thousands of people with two fish and five loaves of bread; He calmed a storm just by speaking to it; He raised Lazarus from the dead; and He conquered sin, sickness, satan, and death through the cross and the resurrection. The miracles of Christ demonstrated that the era of God's salvation had arrived and God's amazing grace continues until this day.

When Jesus ascended into Heaven, He sent the Holy Spirit to empower His people to continue His ministry until He returns. God can use ordinary people in extraordinary ways to accomplish His will and manifest His purposes on the earth. All that God requires of people is their availability. In my Ph.D. dissertation on miracles in the 17th and 18th centuries, I discovered many regular folks who received miraculous answers to their prayers. The early Quakers, for example, testified to the manifestation of a variety of spiritual gifts, including healing, miracles, discerning of spirits, tongues, words of wisdom, and words of knowledge.[4] John Wesley's *Journal* also recorded many supernatural occurrences. My favorite account was of Mary Special who received a dramatic healing of breast cancer.[5] Another woman whose story appears in the *Journal* experienced a release from blindness in her right eye after Jesus Christ appeared to her in a dream.[6] My research taught me that God did not stop working miracles in the first century. He has continued to manifest His power among His people in every age.[7]

In our text, Peter and John encounter a lame man at the temple gate called Beautiful. This was a good place for the man to be, since people on their way to worship would more than likely be inclined to extend generosity to him. The man asks for money, but Peter does not give him what he asks for; he gives him what he actually needs. This is how God works—He often gives us the specific things for which we ask, but He is more concerned about the actual needs in our lives than just the things that we want.

The Lord is gracious, and His desires for us are so much better than what we desire for ourselves. The beggar, because he was lame from birth, probably never thought of the possibility that he would ever walk. However, God wanted to make him whole. God's thoughts are higher than our thoughts, and His ways are higher than our ways. He wants to touch our lives more deeply than we can imagine.

Peter extends God's power to the lame man, and he immediately receives healing through the name of Jesus Christ. The text says in Acts 3:7-8 that Peter:

> *Took him by the right hand and lifted him up, and immediately his feet and ankle bones received strength. So he, leaping up, stood and walked and entered the temple with them—walking, leaping, and praising God.*

The healing of the lame man charges the atmosphere with excitement. The miracle is public, instantaneous, undeniable, and complete. Luke, who wrote the Book of Acts, was a doctor. He therefore gives a thorough and descriptive account of the miracle of healing. If God does something, then His actions can be observed or examined with confidence, by scientists, by doctors, or even by skeptics. Some of you will be physically healed during your individual prayer time or as you study this book. I invite you to allow your doctors to verify your miracle.

As we read further in the Book of Acts, we see that the miracle of healing really shakes up the community and causes quite a bit of controversy among the religious authorities. Yet, the apostles continue to minister in the name of Jesus and are eventually imprisoned. However, the opposition does not stop the advance of the Gospel. Thousands come to know the Lord through the preaching of the Word.

The religious officials are very upset at the spread of the Christian message. Yet, their opposition to the Gospel does not discourage the saints. In fact, the people of God pray for even greater boldness in the preaching of the good news. They pray that God will stretch forth His hand to heal and to perform signs and wonders. In this atmosphere for miracles, the place is shaken, the believers are filled with the Holy Spirit, and they speak the Word of God with boldness. So what do we need to create an atmosphere for miracles? I would like to mention four important things revealed in the text.

First of all, an atmosphere for miracles is created when we exalt the name of Jesus Christ in worship and ministry. Throughout the third and fourth chapters of Acts, the name of Jesus is lifted up, magnified, and reverenced. For example, in Acts 4:12, Peter declares that salvation comes through faith in the name of Jesus Christ. He states:

Nor is there salvation in any other, for there is no other name under heaven given among men by which we must be saved.

The name of Jesus represents the person of Jesus. The name represents all that Jesus is and all that He has. Jesus is the Savior, and He wants to save us in all areas of our lives. He wants to save us spiritually, mentally, emotionally, and physically. He desires to rescue us from sin and spiritual death, fear and guilt, habits and addictions, ignorance and mental illness, satan and demons, despair and emotional bondage, physical sickness, and ultimately even death itself.

The mission of Jesus Christ is about soul salvation, but it is also about whole salvation. Salvation includes everything that makes us whole persons. Salvation includes not only the forgiveness of sins, but also God's protection, peace, healing, deliverance, and general well-being. The name of Jesus represents all that God has for us, and His name, when spoken in faith, based on relationship with Him, will release life-changing power. The well-loved song declares:

Jesus, Jesus, Jesus;
There's just something about that name!
Master, Savior, Jesus,
Like the fragrance after the rain;
Jesus, Jesus, Jesus,
Let all Heaven and earth proclaim;
Kings and kingdoms will all pass away,
But there's something about that name![8]

The name of Jesus is powerful. The name of Jesus gives us the authority to minister effectively. Jesus Christ is the name through which the Gospel is preached and miracles are wrought. Peter says to the lame man in Acts 3:6, *"In the name of Jesus Christ of Nazareth, rise up and walk."* Peter does not speak on the grounds of his own authority but rather on the grounds of the authority of the Son of God. To minister in the name of Jesus is to minister in the same manner as Jesus. It is to minister on behalf of or as an extension of Jesus.

If Jesus Christ physically were present today, He would preach the good news of salvation to us. He would heal the sick, cast out demons, and meet the needs of those He encountered. When we pray for these things, we participate with Jesus to accomplish the work of His Father. To minister in the name of Jesus means to act on His authority so that He receives the glory. Peter says in Acts 4:10:

> *Let it be known to you all, and to all the people of Israel, that by the name of Jesus Christ of Nazareth, whom you crucified, whom God raised from the dead, by Him this man stands here before you whole.*

Peter wants no one to misunderstand how this great miracle has taken place. Jesus Christ is responsible for this wonderful healing, so Peter gives the Lord complete credit for it. When God gives you your miracle, please do not forget to thank Him for it. Please do not forget to give Him the glory and the honor for your individual wholeness. In fact, you do not have to wait for the manifestation of your miracle to express gratitude to God. You can praise Him right now! You can dance in advance. Like Joshua before the walls of Jericho, you can shout before you witness the Lord's saving power! (See Joshua 6 and Hebrews 11:30.)

Second, an atmosphere for miracles requires our faith. Faith is an unshakable trust in the Lord Jesus Christ that causes us to believe and to act on the Word of God. Faith, more than anything else, is about our relationship with God through Jesus Christ. We ask God for lots of things, and there is nothing wrong with asking. Yet, faith is more than the belief that God will do something that we want. Faith is really about the loving relationship that we share with God. Real faith focuses so intently on Jesus Christ that one's problems begin to diminish in comparison to His majesty.

God wants to give us more than the things for which we ask; He wants to give us a relationship with Himself through faith in His Son, Jesus Christ. Real faith has the Lord Jesus Christ as the object of that faith. Of course, we want a blessing or a healing! Of course, we want to escape the problems we are facing, but we must eventually get to the place where Jesus Christ is infinitely more important to us than the things after which we seek. He certainly is going to bless us; He is going to work miracles for us, but we need to appreciate Him simply for who He is. Faith is about our relationship with the Lord.

If we have put our faith in the Lord and are in relationship with Him, then we can live and minister in confidence knowing that God is with us. For Peter to make such a bold proclamation of healing to the lame man, he needed assurance of God's presence and God's endorsement. This assurance was given to him because he had put his full trust in Jesus Christ.

In fact, both Peter and the lame man put their faith in Jesus and His ability to work miracles. Peter had to believe that when he invoked the name of Jesus Christ, the power of God would manifest. The lame man had to believe that his obedient response to Peter's command actually would result in his healing. So both Peter and the lame man exhibited faith. Thus, Peter says in Acts 3:16:

> And [the name of Jesus], *through faith in His name, has made this man strong, whom you see and know. Yes, the faith which comes through Him has given him this perfect soundness in the presence of you all.*

An atmosphere for miracles requires faith in the Lord Jesus Christ. He has the power to do whatever we need.

Some of you may be weak in your faith. Maybe you have experienced a major disappointment in your life or perhaps you have been waiting for many years for a breakthrough. I want to encourage you that God has not forgotten you. He will meet your need at the moment that will bring Him glory and bring you the greatest benefit. Jesus and the disciples had probably passed by the man at the Beautiful Gate many times; however, when Peter and John encountered the man in our text on that particular day, God gave him the miracle that he actually needed. Keep trusting God and He will manifest Himself to you in surprising ways.

Third, an atmosphere for miracles requires prayer. The entire Bible testifies to the importance of prayer. In Second Chronicles 7:14, for example, God declares:

> *If My people who are called by My name will humble themselves, and pray and seek My face, and turn from their wicked ways, then I will hear from heaven, and will forgive their sin and heal their land.*

The New Testament exhorts us to pray without ceasing and to present our petitions to God with joy and thanksgiving. The Book of James teaches us that the prayers of the righteous are powerful and effective. (See First Thessalonians 5:16-18; Philippians 4:6; James 5:16.) Prayer is one of the most important Christian activities.

The magnificent story of healing in our text begins with Peter and John going to the temple to pray. It ends with the believers praying for boldness to preach the Gospel. Their prayers are so powerful that the place where they are gathered is shaken. We need to commit ourselves to this type of intensity in prayer! Prayer is the way in which we receive many of the good things that God has for us. I challenge you to reach out to God in prayer and to trust Him to work a miracle in your life.

Fourth and finally, an atmosphere for miracles is created as we are filled with the Holy Spirit. Acts 4:31 says of the believers:

> *When they had prayed, the place where they were assembled together was shaken; and they were all filled with the Holy Spirit, and they spoke the word of God with boldness.*

To be filled with the Holy Spirit is simply to be guided and controlled by Him. The Holy Spirit leads, strengthens, teaches, and empowers God's people. This empowerment is known as the Baptism in the Holy Spirit. After a person receives salvation, he or she continually must yield to the Holy Spirit in order to do the works of God with greater effectiveness. The Lord will equip the believer to meet the various needs of the Body of Christ. Two possible results of Spirit Baptism include: (1) holy boldness and (2) the emergence of spiritual gifts, such as tongues, prophecy, discernment, healings, and miracles.

Whatever we do for God becomes more effective when we yield ourselves to the Holy Spirit and allow Him to empower us. Jesus said in Acts 1:8:

> *But you shall receive power when the Holy Spirit has come upon you; and you shall be witnesses to Me in Jerusalem, and in all Judea and Samaria, and to the end of the earth.*

The power of the Holy Spirit absolutely is necessary for Christian ministry. The Lord wants to do many exciting things through you. Commit yourself to His service and ask Him to fill you with His Spirit.

EVEN NOW, THE LORD HAS THE POWER TO WORK A MIRACLE: TRUSTING IN GOD'S TIMING

The raising of Lazarus from the dead teaches us a lot about the timing of God in meeting the needs of human beings. In John 11:1-44, we see an impressive demonstration of the love of God and the resurrection power of Jesus Christ. The Lord, after a delay of several days, raises His friend Lazarus from the dead.

In the text, Jesus hears the news that His close friend Lazarus of the city of Bethany is sick. Lazarus is the brother of Mary and Martha. Many of you will remember Mary and Martha from Luke 10. Mary, the younger sister, sits and learns at Jesus' feet.

Martha, on the other hand, worries so much about being a gracious host that she neglects spending time with the Lord. John adds concerning Mary that she is the one who anointed Jesus with fragrant oil and wiped His feet with her hair.

Jesus says in John 11:4, *"This sickness is not unto death, but for the glory of God, that the Son of God may be glorified through it."* We know that Lazarus does in fact die before the Lord reaches Bethany, so what does Jesus mean by the statement, *"This sickness is not unto death"?* I believe that Jesus simply is seeing the end from the beginning. He sees that the result of this tragic episode will be one of victory over death, so He prophesies God's perspective over the situation. Christ reveals that the purpose of Lazarus' sickness is not death, but the glorification of the Son of God. Presumably, God allows the sickness so that He can reveal compassion through the actions of His Son, Jesus Christ.

After the Lord hears about the problem, He does something that we all have probably seen in our own lives—He delays solving the problem. He stays two more days where He is located. Sometimes there is a considerable amount of time between the prophecy and the fulfillment. Jesus does not hurry to Bethany. He does not stop what He is doing in order to rescue Lazarus. Christ does not even choose to speak the Word in order to heal His friend from a distance!

The Lord's timing and priorities are often very different from ours. Isaiah 55:8 puts the issue quite clearly: *"'For My thoughts are not your thoughts, neither are your ways My ways,' says the Lord."* Now I must admit that sometimes the Lord's timing is quite frustrating to me. It is difficult to wait on the Lord when financial or other kinds of deadlines are rapidly approaching. When I am in trouble, I want the problem to be solved immediately. I want the Lord to rush into my situation blowing a trumpet! I want Him to kick the door in and proclaim, "Help is here!" However, the Lord rarely responds the moment that we get into trouble. He is seldom early and often seems quite late when we need Him.

I can imagine what Mary and Martha must have said to one another:

> Where is Jesus? When is He going to arrive? We hope that He gets here soon! He knows that Lazarus is sick. God, please help Lazarus to get better! Where is Jesus?

The sisters wait eagerly for the Lord's arrival and then the unthinkable happens. Jesus does not get to Bethany in time to heal the sickness, and Lazarus dies! There was no 11th-hour miracle, not even a 12th-hour miracle! Lazarus dies, he is buried, and he remains in the tomb for four days. From the human perspective, all possible hope is gone! However, the Lord has the final word. I want to encourage you with that truth—the Lord has the final word! Some of you have been praying for a long time and crying out to the Lord for a breakthrough. It seems like your 11th hours and 12th hours have passed, and I am sure that you have asked the question, "When is the Lord going to show up in my situation?"

Child of God, regardless of what the circumstances may suggest, the Lord has not forgotten you. He loves you; He cares for you; and He is going to meet you at your point of need. Your suffering has not been in vain. The Lord is going to work out that impossible situation for you. He is going to transform your tragedy into triumph. Trust Him today. I love the following beautiful words of encouragement:

> God is too wise to be mistaken.
> God is too good to be unkind.
> So when you don't understand,
> When you don't see His plan,
> When you can't trace His hand, trust His heart.[9]

175

The Lord is not unmindful of our trials; He just has His unique perspective of them. He wants us to learn to trust Him in all circumstances. He is going to help us at just the right time. God's will and timing are perfect. When things happen according to God's will and in God's timing, He gets the glory and we receive the maximum benefit. God responds to every cry for help, but in His own time and on His own terms.

When Jesus finally arrives on the scene of tragedy near the outskirts of Bethany, He encounters His friend Martha. She says to Him in John 11:21, *"Lord, if You had been here, my brother would not have died."* Her statement is not necessarily one of anger, but of fact. She acknowledges her trust in Jesus' ability to heal. She knows that Christ could have prevented Lazarus from dying had the Lord been present at the time of sickness.

Martha expresses her trust further in verse 22. She says with confidence, *"But even now I know that whatever You ask of God, God will give You."* "But even now" is a cry of faith; it is a cry of trust in the Lord Jesus Christ. Martha does not realize the magnitude of the miracle that she is about to witness. However, she does know that the Lord cares for her and that He is going to bring the power of God into her situation.

Notice that Martha says to Jesus, *"But even now I know that whatever You ask of God, God will give You."* Martha trusts Christ to petition the Father for the right thing. The Lord Jesus Christ is our advocate with the Father in the divine court of justice and mercy. He now intercedes for us at the right hand of the Father. We must learn to surrender our prayer requests to the Lord. It is OK to be specific with our petitions; however, the Lord may refine them so that they more perfectly line up with the will of His Father. First John 5:14-15 reads as follows:

> *Now this is the confidence that we have in Him, that if*
> *we ask anything according to His will, He hears us. And*

*if we know that He hears us, whatever we ask, we know
that we have the petitions that we have asked of Him.*

It is God's will to provide for our needs. God is going to give
us exactly the things that will lead to our highest good; however,
sometimes our needs and our wants are different. Sometimes the
thing that we want is not the thing that we need. Sometimes the
thing that we want may be a good thing, but our timing does not
coincide with the Lord's timing. For example, had Jesus come earlier than He did and prevented Lazarus from dying, He would not
have had the opportunity to glorify God through the demonstration of resurrection power. The Lord knows the best time and the
best manner to show up in our situation, and when He shows up,
as my dad always says, "He is going to show out!"

In John 11:23, Jesus communicates to Martha the will of the
Heavenly Father. He says to her, *"Your brother will rise again."*
She replies to Him in verse 24, *"I know that he will rise again in
the resurrection at the last day."* Martha understands that Lazarus will indeed be raised to life in the future, but she does not
have the expectation that Jesus will do a present miracle of resurrection. Therefore, Martha's faith is underdeveloped. She believes
in Jesus Christ. She even believes in His ability to heal and to
prevent death. However, she does not have a full appreciation of
His power over death.

Jesus responds to Martha, *"I am the resurrection and the
life."* The Lord challenges Martha to see His "nowness." Christ
not only makes resurrection possible in the future, He is the resurrection and the life, right now. The giver and sustainer of life
now stands before Martha, and He challenges her to see and to
embrace His fullness.

The Lord continues, *"He who believes in Me, though he may
die, he shall live and whoever lives and believes in Me shall never
die."* Christ offers eternal life to those who believe in Him. If a be-

liever dies physically, he or she one day will rise from the dead and will live again for all eternity. Moreover, since it is true that the one who believes in Jesus and dies will live again for all eternity, then no believer will ever die ultimately. Death then for the believer is only a temporary foe. Death is not the final stop for the believer.

After Martha encounters the Lord, she goes to get her sister, Mary. When Mary sees the Lord, she responds to Him in the same manner as her sister Martha had responded earlier. She falls down at the feet of the Master and says to Him, *"Lord, if You had been here, my brother would not have died."* Mary's weeping and the pain that she and the others feel touch the heart of Jesus. Verse 33 states that Jesus groans in His spirit and is troubled. Verse 35 adds that Jesus weeps as He approaches the tomb of Lazarus. So why does Jesus weep when He knows that He is going to raise Lazarus from the dead? I believe that Jesus weeps because His heart is full of love and compassion. The Lord's weeping reveals His humanity to us. Even though Jesus Christ is fully God, He is also fully human. He weeps for us. He feels what we feel. He knows our pain. He understands the full range of human experience. As Hebrews 4:15 reminds us, "[He can] *be touched with the feeling of our infirmities"* (KJV).

Jesus, full of love, compassion, and intense emotion, says in John 11:39, *"Take away the stone."* Martha, with her underdeveloped faith, replies, *"Lord, by this time there is a stench, for he has been dead four days."* Martha still does not quite appreciate the fact that she is in the very presence of the resurrection and the life. Time is not an obstacle for the Son of God. I can relate to Martha, though. Sometimes faith falters in the face of the facts. Martha is human, after all. However, Martha's trust in Jesus Christ is going to see her through. Even now, the Lord has the power to work a miracle! Jesus says to Martha in verse 40, *"Did I not say to you that if you would believe you would see the glory of God?"* Martha, Mary, the disciples, and everyone present are about to witness the resurrection power of Jesus Christ!

The stone in front of Lazarus's tomb is removed and Jesus begins to speak to the Heavenly Father in verse 41. He says with confidence, *"Father, I thank You that You have heard Me."* If the Father has heard Jesus, then this means that Jesus has already prayed about the situation. Christ can now respond to the Father with words of thanksgiving rather than words of petition. Jesus' prayer life is a model for us that demonstrates the Lord's close bond with His Father. Christ lives in constant communion with His Father and always operates according to the Father's will. Jesus has infinite power Himself, but His power always operates within the context of His obedient, loving, and trusting relationship with God the Father. If we, like Jesus, will pursue a relationship with God and commit ourselves to His divine plans and purposes, then we too will experience freedom and confidence in our prayer times.

Jesus continues His prayer of assurance in verse 42. He says boldly to His Father: *"I know that You always hear Me, but because of the people who are standing by I said this, that they may believe that You sent Me."*

Martha had said to the Lord in verse 27, *"Yes, Lord, I believe that You are the Christ, the Son of God, who is to come into the world."* Her faith in Christ is already firmly established at this point. However, Jesus wants everyone who witnesses the miracle to come to faith in Him.

In verse 43, Jesus cries out with one of the most powerful commands in the New Testament. He says, *"Lazarus, come forth!"* It does not take a bunch of words for Christ to get the job done. When the Lord speaks to a situation, it has to change. The story concludes with Lazarus coming out of the tomb. Death is no match for the very Lord of life. The text reads:

> *And he who had died came out bound hand and foot with graveclothes, and his face was wrapped with a cloth. Jesus said to them, "Loose him, and let him go."*

The story of Lazarus has encouraged the people of God for centuries. The very name *Lazarus* means "God helps." He is an ever-present help in times of trouble (see Ps. 46:1). If the Lord raised Lazarus from the dead with just a single command, then He can speak a word into your life and fix any situation that you are facing. In addition, whatever God has placed in your heart at any time in your past can be raised to new life again. Even now, you can start a business. Even now, you can buy a home. Even now, you can finish your college degree. Even now, you can begin a new career. Even now, the Lord has the power to revive you and to sustain you into your destiny. I challenge you to put your trust in Him so that you will see the glory of God. I challenge you to believe Him today for a resurrection miracle in your life. It is never too late.

The closest personal example of resurrection that I can cite is God's sparing of my mother's life in 2008. My mother Glendolyn was hospitalized on the 26th of July (her birthday) with severe high blood pressure and complications from dialysis. By that evening, she was on a ventilator and unconscious. She remained in that state for several days. It took me about four days to get to Georgia from California, but God gave me an inner assurance that my mother would pull through, as I prayed for her recovery. By Friday, she was off the ventilator and eating a chef's salad. One physician attributed the recovery to my family's faith in God. Another physician remarked, "You are connected to a higher source of healing than our medicine." God still works miracles today!

The raising of Lazarus was a sign of something greater to come. A short time after Jesus performed this awesome miracle, He died on the cross and rose from the dead Himself. As great a miracle as was the raising of Lazarus, far greater was the resurrection of Jesus Christ. Lazarus would die again; Jesus would never die again. When Jesus Christ rose from the dead, He conquered sin, sickness, satan, and death. He now offers eternal life to us and ensures us that one day we shall experience resurrection and never see death again. Until that glorious day, we humbly can pursue all that God has for us in this life. He graciously extends to us His love and power in order to save us in every area of our lives. In His perfect timing, He will make us whole.

EXPECT A MIRACLE IN YOUR LIFE

We cannot demand miracles from God, but we can expect Him to work miracles when He deems them necessary. God works both in spectacular and nonspectacular ways to accomplish His purposes. We can wait for Him in confidence and expect Him to meet our needs when the time is right. Furthermore, no challenge is too difficult for Him. God can heal any type of disease. He can recreate a nonfunctioning organ. Financial breakthroughs are no problem for Him. God can provide wisdom for situations that are humanly impossible. He can come through when natural deadlines have come and gone.

When I was a senior in high school, I failed to apply for an engineering scholarship offered by AT&T Bell Laboratories. The scholarship had certain requirements that I thought disqualified me from consideration, so I did not research any of its particulars. I soon forgot about the scholarship and began to shift my focus to completing my final year. Sometime later, my mom decided to take a music course at the local college. She befriended one of her fellow classmates, and they often talked about various topics related to family and other things. In one conversation, my mom mentioned that I was doing well in school and soon would be attending Massachusetts Institute of Technology. My mom's friend mentioned that she knew someone who worked for AT&T who might be interested in providing me with a summer internship, so my mom passed my information along to her friend.

Several weeks later, I received in the mail a scholarship application from AT&T Bell Labs. Unfortunately, it arrived about a month after the stated deadline; however, I decided to complete it anyway. Another several weeks passed, and I received a phone call from someone on the scholarship committee who interviewed me about my plans for college. The next day, the committee member called me again and informed me that I was a scholarship recipient. At that point, I still did not know exactly what the scholarship would cover. I assumed that it would provide a few thousand dollars for college and possibly a summer job. I asked the committee member for more details about the scholarship and he informed me that it was comprehensive. It covered tuition, room, board, books, and a summer internship. My entire education at MIT would be paid in full!

God's provision for my college education was indeed miraculous. He worked through a sequence of circumstances in order to bless me in an extraordinary way. Even my mistakes and lack of follow-through did not frustrate God's plans for my education. He had the whole situation under control. I learned from the experience that God indeed orders the steps of His people. He will work miracles if necessary to accomplish His purposes.

As I conclude this chapter, I would like to encourage you to trust God in whatever difficult situations that you find yourself. God is with you. Even if He does not respond in the manner that you are hoping for, He will meet you in ways that will bring wholeness to you at deeper levels. Healing, for example, can happen at a spiritual or emotional level, even when it does not occur at a physical level. God cares about the total person, and He has a divine sequence of things that He wants to do in your life. Allow Him to address your problems in the order that will benefit you the most. God's will and priorities ultimately will lead to your greatest good.

A PRAYER FOR A MIRACLE

Father, I praise Your holy name and the name of Your Son, Jesus Christ. I put my full trust in You and renew my commitment to Your will. I ask You to forgive my sins and to cleanse me of all unrighteousness. I accept Your forgiveness and cleansing. Fill me, O Lord, with the precious Holy Spirit and Holy Spirit, I ask You to empower this time of petition. Reproduce within my life Christian character and conformity to the will of the Father.

Dear God, I am facing a particularly difficult situation in my life right now. [Elaborate on your specific need(s).] *Yet, I know that the things that are impossible with men are possible with You. Therefore, I petition You, O God, to extend Your mighty hand of grace to me to work a miracle on my behalf. I need You to* [some examples: heal my body of cancer, provide a financial breakthrough in my life, restore my marriage, rescue my child from drug addiction, etc.]. *You are a God who works miracles. You created the universe out of nothing. You have healed the sick and even raised the dead. I know that You love me and that You are on my side, so I ask You to help me in this situation. The story of Lazarus teaches me that it is never too late to receive a miracle from You.*

Dear God, I cannot command or coerce You into doing my will, but I can trust in Your infinite liberality and generosity. Please work out this situation for me by Your great power. I adjust my heart and thinking to receive the help that Your mighty hand extends to me.

I now speak to any mountain that opposes Your will and command it to be thrown into the sea. I trust that You have worked out the situation for my good, and I await Your favor, Your timing, and Your instruction. In the name of the Lord Jesus Christ, I pray. Amen.

Chapter Summary

1. The church continues the ministry of Jesus Christ through the working of miracles.

2. The healing of the lame man at the Beautiful Gate led to thousands of conversions.

3. An atmosphere for miracles is created when:

    • We exalt the name of Jesus Christ in worship and ministry.

    • We put our faith in Jesus Christ.

    • We pray.

    • We are filled with the Holy Spirit.

4. The raising of Lazarus teaches us that God is never too late. Miracles can remove the limitation of timing.

Reflection/Discussion Questions

1. What new insights did you receive from reading this chapter?

2. Have you ever witnessed a miracle like the healing of the lame man?

3. Why does God perform miracles?

4. Why does God sometimes choose not to perform miracles?

5. Why did Jesus wait so long to raise Lazarus from the dead? Do you sometimes feel as if God is taking too long to answer your prayers?

6. What comfort does this chapter give you concerning God's timing?

PRACTICAL APPLICATIONS AND ACTIVITIES

1. Locate several passages in the Bible that speak of miracles. Record these in a journal.

2. Tell a family member or friend about what you learned in this chapter.

3. Write out your own prayer for a miracle. Share it with someone.

Chapter 8

Wholeness Through the Discipline of Prayer

We look upon prayer simply as a means of getting things for ourselves, but the biblical purpose of prayer is that we may get to know God Himself.

—Oswald Chambers[1]

The Fundamental Requirement of Effective Prayer

These things I have written to you who believe in the name of the Son of God, that you may know that you have eternal life, and that you may continue to believe in the name of the Son of God. Now this is the confidence that we have in Him, that if we ask anything according to His will, He hears us. And if we know that He hears us, whatever we ask, we know that we have the petitions that we have asked of Him (1 John 5:13-15).[2]

If we are going to experience God's salvation and wholeness in our lives, then we must learn to pray effectively. Prayer is just talking to God, or better yet, talking *with* God. To pray is to engage in meaningful conversation with the Living God. I define prayer as personal communion and communication with God. Prayer is a worship activity. Through prayer, we worship and fellowship with God. God reveals His character, His will, His ways, and His power to us as we seek Him. We gain an intimate knowledge of who God is and what He expects of us. We come to know by experience that God is good and that He loves us with an everlasting love. Through prayer, we also learn to yield ourselves to God. God shows us the things about our lives that please Him and that displease Him. He also enables us to become more like Christ in our character and actions.

Through consistent prayer, we receive God's direction. God will teach us what to do in the various situations of life that we face. Jesus said that His sheep would listen to His voice and follow Him (see John 10). Guidance is one of the principal provisions of God that we receive through prayer. God speaks to us primarily through the Bible. He may also speak to us through prophecy or through other gifts of the Holy Spirit. Sometimes God places an answer in our minds as we quiet ourselves before Him. We cannot dictate to God how to communicate with us, but God will speak to us when we take the time to listen to Him.

Through prayer, God meets our needs. Jesus taught us to pray, *"Give us this day our daily bread"* (Matt. 6:11). God is our Provider. He is our Shepherd, and He will never withhold any good thing from us. We can pray to the Father with confidence concerning the things that we need because Jesus gives us the authority to approach Him. In Christ, we have full access to God's presence, power, and provision.

Finally, through prayer, God allows us to cooperate with His divine will. In other words, prayer changes things. Prayer can move mountains. Prayer can bring physical and emotional healing. Prayer can lead to deliverance from demonic opposition. Jesus Christ said in Matthew 19:26, *"With God all things are pos-*

sible." God can do anything, except fail. If we pray according to God's will, there is nothing that He will not do for us.

The fundamental requirement of effective prayer is to pray according to the will of God. God wills for us to worship Him with pure hearts. He wills for us to seek Him with diligence and serve Him with excellence. God wills for us to resist the enemy. He wills for us to love one another, to reach lost souls, and to represent Him in all that we do. God also wills for each of us to flourish in every area of our lives and to become the men and women that He has created us to be. As we submit to the will and purposes of God, He will provide us with many unexpected benefits and He will bless us according to His riches in glory by Christ Jesus (see Phil. 4:19).

Let us now examine First John 5:13-15 more closely. The apostle states in verse 13 that the purpose of his entire letter is to provide assurance to believers of the eternal life that we possess through belief in Jesus Christ. He states:

> *These things I have written to you who believe in the name of the Son of God, that you may know that you have eternal life, and that you may continue to believe in the name of the Son of God.*

To pray in the name of Jesus is to pray on the grounds of His authority. To pray in the name of Jesus is to pray as Jesus Himself would pray. It is to approach God on the merits of what Jesus Christ did at Calvary. It is to act as an ambassador for the King of kings and the Lord of lords. If Jesus Christ physically were present today, He would extend His salvation to us; He would bless our marriages; He would minister to our children; He would meet our needs. When we pray for these things, we participate with Jesus to accomplish the work of His Father.

The name of Jesus gives us full access to God. The name of Jesus gives us the authority to approach the Heavenly Father to receive every spiritual blessing that He has provided for us (see Eph. 1:3). The name of Jesus represents the fullness of all that God is and all that He has. Jesus Christ is the Son of God. He is the Alpha and the Omega. He is our Lord and Savior. He is our Blessed Redeemer. He is the Bread of Life, the Living Water, and the Good Shepherd. He is the Friend that sticks closer than a brother does. He is the Great Physician, the Author and the Finisher of our Faith, and the Prince of Peace. Jesus Christ is everything we need. His mighty name assures us that He is greater than any and every challenge we face!

We believe in the name of Jesus to receive eternal life, the Holy Spirit, physical healing, and every good and perfect gift from the Father. In John 16:23, Jesus said to His disciples, *"Whatever you ask the Father in My name He will give you."* Prayer is a beautiful thing. Prayer is the way that God allows us to commune with Him. God is not trying to find out what our needs are. Jesus said that the Father already knows our needs before we ask Him (see Matt. 6:8). Although it is certainly biblical to bring our needs to God, His greatest desire is for us to know Him better. He wants to reveal His heart to us. He wants us to know His ways and to surrender our selfish desires and ambitions to Him so that He can make us whole.

If the general purpose of prayer is fellowship with God, then one specific goal of prayer is conformity to the will of God. To pray in Jesus' name and to pray according to the will of God both mean the same thing. When we yield our wills to God, we enter into a partnership with Him. Through prayer, God gives us the privilege of helping Him to accomplish His purposes on earth. This is why Jesus taught us to pray, *"Your kingdom come. Your will be done on earth as it is in heaven"* (Matt. 6:10). Prayer is one mechanism that God uses to bring the natural realm into alignment with the spiritual realm.

First John 5:14 states, *"Now this is the confidence that we have in Him, that if we ask anything according to His will, He hears us."* God listens to those who are in a relationship with Him. Those who are in a relationship with God, who are abiding in His Word, who are obeying His commands, and who are trusting in His name can address the Father with the confidence that He is listening to them.

Not only does God listen to those who are committed to His will, but He also listens favorably to their requests. This is because those who pray according to the will of God want the same things that God wants. Prayer is not a way of bending God's will to our will; prayer is a way of subordinating our will to God's will.[3] "When we learn to want what God wants, we have the joy of receiving the answer to our petitions."[4] David puts the issue quite plainly in Psalm 37:4. There he says, *"Delight yourself also in the Lord, and He shall give you the desires of your heart."*

First John 5:15 continues: *"And if we know that He hears us, whatever we ask, we know that we have the petitions that we have asked of Him."*

In other words, since we know that God hears us each time that we ask in His will, then we also know with equal certainty that He grants the requests we have made the precise moment that we prayed. This promise in First John 5 reminds me of the words found in Isaiah 65:24. There God declares, *"It shall come to pass that before they call, I will answer; and while they are still speaking, I will hear."*

The apostle John in our text also seems to be echoing the words of Jesus found in Mark 11:24. Christ said in Mark 11:24, *"Therefore I say to you, whatever things you ask when you pray, believe that you receive them, and you will have them."* When we pray according to the Father's will, we know that we have our requests because God certainly is going to accomplish His own

191

plans and purposes. All we are actually doing is jumping onto God's bandwagon. We yield ourselves to God so that His glory can be revealed in us and we can become physical channels of His love, mercy, and power.

The surrender of our wills to the will of the Father brings joy and freedom to our prayer lives. When we surrender to God, He guides and directs us how to pray and for what to pray. He places His thoughts and instructions into our minds so that we can communicate His desires through our words. Prayer truly is cooperation between God and us.

The life of prayer is a walk of faith. God requires His people to put their faith in Him. He desires for us to trust in His willingness and ability to handle every situation that we encounter in the manner and the timing that He deems necessary. God sees the whole picture. He wants only what is best for us. When we surrender to His will, He gets the glory and we receive the maximum benefit.

The way to know the will of God is to stay in His Word. The more we read, hear, meditate on, and embrace the truth of God's Word, the stronger our faith will become and the quicker we will come into alignment with God's perfect will. Jesus said in John 15:7, *"If you abide in Me, and My words abide in you, you will ask what you desire, and it shall be done for you."* When the Word of God gets down on the inside of us, when it settles in our spirits, when it becomes a part of us, then God's desires become our desires. Our prayers will be effective because we have come into agreement with God. When we are in agreement with God, then we can pray with boldness, confidence, assurance, power, and intensity. When we are in agreement with God, we can expect Him to move mightily, to work miracles, to heal bodies, to mend marriages, to provide finances, and to meet our needs. We can expect God to accomplish everything that He wills to accomplish in our lives, in our churches, in our cities, in this nation, and in the whole world. I have often witnessed hundreds of souls come into the Kingdom during a single church service because the people of God dared to come into agreement with Him and declare His salvation.

DISCERNING THE WILL OF GOD

It is essential that we discover the purposes and plans of God for our lives, families, ministries, vocations, decisions, and everything else that concerns us. Prayer is essential to discerning the will of God. Prayer is communication, and all real communication involves listening. The listening side of prayer is probably more important than the vocal side. Some Christians are so used to talking and giving laundry lists of requests to God that they fail to take time to receive instructions from Him. God will speak to us when we take the time to listen to Him.

Proverbs 3:5-6 declares:

Trust in the Lord with all your heart and lean not on your own understanding; in all your ways acknowledge Him, and He will make your paths straight.

James 1:5 says,

If any of you lacks wisdom, he should ask God, who gives generously to all without finding fault, and it will be given to him (NIV).

Many other Bible verses speak about God's responses to us, but my point is that God has committed Himself to providing us with the important answers that we need from Him.

There is no formula for hearing God. We cannot force God to say something to us or coerce God into moving in a certain way. Listening to God happens within the context of our loving relationship with Him. God will communicate with us because He loves us and desires that we know His will.

The Bible is the primary instrument through which God communicates to His people (see Josh. 1:8; Ps. 37:31; 119:105,130; 2 Tim. 3:16-17). Any spiritual direction that we receive from any source should be in agreement with the Bible. The Bible is the written Word of God. It tells us how to have a strong relationship with God. It gives us instruction on what is right and wrong. It also describes what God wants from us and how we are to draw closer to Him. The Bible is our final authority. There is no higher knowledge of God to which we have access than the Bible. Our response to the written Word of God should be simple obedience (see James 1:22).

Mental assent to the truth of the Word is not enough; we must be doers of the Word. That is, we must put the Word of God into practice. Jesus said in Luke 11:28, *"Blessed are those who hear the word of God and keep it."* He also said in John 15:14, *"You are My friends if you do whatever I command you."* There are many commands in the Bible. We are to love God and others; we are to turn away from sexual immorality, etc. We can agree that these things are important, but our embrace of the message of the Bible requires obedience to what it tells us to do. We must obey the things that we read.

A single-minded commitment to God and His Word increases our sensitivity to Him. Jeremiah 29:13 declares, *"And you will seek Me and find Me, when you search for Me with all your heart."* The opposite of single-mindedness is double-mindedness (see James 1:5-8). Double-mindedness is a state of split allegiance, a state of halfhearted commitment to God. When James writes about doubting, he is talking about the issue of divided loyalties. The person with a double mind is not interested in trusting God or in being in relationship with God. The double-minded person is only interested in playing it safe. He or she sends up prayers just in case they might help, but with no real sense of expectation. The storms of opposition and persecution constantly threaten that person's commitment to God. As human beings, we all have mental reservations and moments of weakness. Abraham was a man of great faith, but he also made major mistakes. Yet, Abraham was committed to God. Even though we all will make mistakes in life, let us never wane in our commitment to God. A committed heart is open to receive instruction from God.

The Bible, God's primary instrument of revelation to humankind, also recounts several other methods of divine communication. For example, God sometimes communicates directly to His people (e.g., see Exod. 3:4; Acts 9:3-4; 1 Kings 19:11; John 16:13). We should not expect God to speak audibly to us today, though, because He has already revealed in the Bible the main things that we need to know about Him and about the Christian walk. Several other ways that God may speak to us in our personal lives when we need specific guidance are listed below.

- God speaks through wise counsel (see Prov. 11:14). God can speak to us through others. For this reason, we should always surround ourselves with godly individuals who are seeking the will of God themselves.

- God speaks through peace (see Phil. 4:6-9). When we pray and seek God though prayer and with an attitude of humility, we will receive a "peace" concerning what to do. God will give us assurance that He is directing our steps.

- God speaks through His character. Often we can discern whether something is God's will by whether or not it lines up with God's character. Of course, we discover God's character through His Word and through relationship with Him.

- God speaks through prophecies, dreams, visions, and spiritual gifts (see Acts 2:17; 1 Cor. 12:4-11). God has very dramatic ways of speaking at times; however, the Word of God must judge all human experiences.

God will find creative ways to speak to us. When He does, we can recognize His voice by its authority and love. There are several ways we can increase our sensitivity to God. First, we need to daily repent of our sins. Sin blocks our receptivity to the leading of the Holy Spirit. Second, we need to meditate on the Word. To meditate on the Word is to rehearse it mentally and verbally. It is to think deeply about what we read so that the message of Scripture becomes personal to us. Joshua 1:8 declares:

This Book of the Law shall not depart from your mouth, but you shall meditate in it day and night, that you may observe to do according to all that is written in it. For then you will make your way prosperous, and then you will have good success.

We need to keep God's Word in our thoughts and on our lips. Third, to increase our sensitivity to God, we should quiet ourselves before Him. Jesus often retreated to solitary places to pray (see Mark 1:35; Luke 5:16). Quietness in prayer reduces emotional intensity and enables us more quickly to discern the will of God. I have discovered, for example, that God's wisdom during crises usually comes to me two or three days after I pray, when my emotions have had time to settle down. Lastly, God often responds to an attitude of expectation. He rewards those who diligently seek Him (see Heb. 11:6). Therefore, we must come before Him in prayer with confidence and trust.

How can we discern whether a message is from God, our minds, or satan? First, God will never violate the Bible. Any message that contradicts the Bible is not from God. Any message that condones sin, fuels pride, or incites confusion is not from God. Also, God always glorifies Himself and edifies His people. If a message is destructive, unloving, unkind, condemning, etc., then it is not from God. God corrects and chastens us, but He always does His work in a spirit of love. Sometimes God's processes are inconvenient, or even painful, but ultimately, they are for our good.

During my early days of seminary, I experienced several months of financial hardship and often felt that God was taking an awfully long time to lead me to the right employment, although I knew that He had directed me to Southern California. With the benefit of hindsight, I can clearly see that God was working behind the scenes to prepare a special place of blessing for me. Not only did He provide me with adequate income (I soon forgot about my financial woes), but He also brought people into my life who would become lifelong friends. God's favor was worth the wait! His Word can be trusted regardless of difficult circumstances. Obeying His voice will always lead to what is best.

Second, when we pray about our relationships with other people, we must remember that God always seeks to bring reconciliation. God does not tear down others with whom we have disagreements. Even when other people wrong us, God usually requires that we make extra efforts to love them. God does not tolerate unforgiveness, bitterness, backbiting, and strife.

Third, God's voice always challenges us to become more like Him. Because we are not perfect, we continually must learn, grow, develop, and refine our actions. We never reach a place in which this process of spiritual maturity becomes unnecessary. If the "voice" that you are hearing does not challenge you to become more like God, then it is not from Him.

Finally, God's voice always produces good results or good fruit. It will strengthen, edify, and enlighten. It will bring encouragement, joy, and peace. It will bring thoughts of compassion toward others. It will bring loving correction. It will bring confidence and hope, and it will inspire and sustain faith. Ultimately, God's voice will glorify the Lord Jesus Christ. God's voice always produces good results.

Before I conclude this section, I want to remind you that God has not left you alone during your times of prayer. God has given the Holy Spirit to His people to help us to pray correctly. Romans 8:26 declares:

> *Likewise the Spirit also helps in our weaknesses. For we do not know what we should pray for as we ought, but the Spirit Himself makes intercession for us with groanings which cannot be uttered.*

Jude 20 encourages us to pray in the Holy Spirit (see also John 4:23-24; Gal. 4:6; Eph. 6:18). To pray in the Spirit is to pray under the inspiration of the Holy Spirit, under the control of the Holy Spirit, or under the direction of the Holy Spirit. Without the Spirit's guidance, we easily can become self-centered in our praying.

Another meaning of "praying in the Spirit" is praying in tongues (see 1 Cor. 14:15-16). There are particular benefits to praying in tongues. Some of these benefits include edification, greater awareness of God's presence, stimulation of faith, and activation of spiritual gifts. On this last point, I have observed that praying in tongues stirs up physical gifts of healings. Oftentimes, as I have prayed for the sick and not received a word of knowledge about the details of a sickness, I have simply placed my hands on the sick person and prayed in tongues. Usually, there is some physical manifestation of God's presence (like heat) during these times and some level of healing takes place. So praying in tongues is one of several ways to pray in the Spirit.

Praying in the Spirit is not limited to tongues, though. Tongues are not a substitute for careful study, preparation, and other spiritual disciplines. Whenever God guides our praying, which should always be the case, we are praying in the Spirit. When we offer up intelligent prayers to God that agree with His revealed will in the Scriptures, then we also are praying in the Spirit. We can pray in tongues or we can pray with understanding. Allow the Holy Spirit to direct you in your prayer times and to lead you to the wholeness that you seek.

SAMPLE PRAYERS FOR WISDOM

Below are a few examples of prayers for wisdom and direction from the Scriptures. These prayers may serve as models for you in your petitioning of God for His divine guidance and help.

- First Kings 3 (especially verses 5-9) and Second Chronicles 1 (especially verses 7-10)—Solomon asks for wisdom to lead God's people and to discern between right and wrong.

- Second Chronicles 20:1-30 (especially verses 6-12)—Jehoshaphat calls upon the Lord for wisdom and help against the people of Ammon, Moab, and Mount Seir. Note verse 12, *"We do not know what to do, but our eyes are upon You"* (NIV).

- Ephesians 1:17-20—Paul prays for the Ephesians to receive the Spirit of wisdom and revelation.

- Colossians 1:9—Paul prays for the Colossians to receive knowledge of God's will.

Here is another example of a prayer for wisdom based on the Scriptures. It illustrates how the Word of God informs our communication with Him. When we find ourselves at a loss for words during prayer, we can always pray the Scriptures. We can rest assured that such scriptural prayers are consistent with God's will. As such, God hears them and will grant our petition for wisdom (see 1 John 5:14-15).

Heavenly Father, I uplift Your holy name. I praise You because You are God Almighty and I thank You for every good and perfect gift that You have given me (see James 1:17), especially the gift of Your Son, Jesus Christ. Father, Your Word declares that if anyone lacks wisdom, he or she should ask of God who gives generously to all without finding fault (see James 1:5). Therefore, dear God, with humility, reverence, and openness I petition You for Your wisdom concerning this situation that I am facing. I do not know what to do, but my eyes are upon You (see 2 Chron. 20:12). The situation is a difficult one, and I am completely dependent on You for help. Yet, I know, O God, that You are greater than every challenge that I face. You are bigger than my circumstances and greater than my trials. As such, I can trust You fully; I can place my entire situation in Your loving hands and cast my care upon You (see 1 Pet. 5:7). I can wait for Your wisdom and guidance with confidence, without wavering, and without fear (see James 1:6-8).

Thank You, God, for being an ever-present help in trouble (see Ps. 46:1). Thank You for being my rock, my refuge, my strength and my friend (see Ps. 18). Thank You that Your compassion, Your mercy, and Your steadfast love that never fails (see Lam. 3:22ff.). Help me to remain faithful even in the midst of difficult challenges. Help me to maintain Christian joy as I face the trials and difficulties of life (see James 1:2), because in these trials You are helping me to develop perseverance and to become mature (see James 1:4). Finally, dear God, as Paul prayed concerning the Ephesians and the Colossians, give to me a spirit of wisdom and revelation that I may know You better. Give me a greater knowledge of who You are and what Your will is (see Eph. 1:17ff; Col. 1:9). Help me to see things from Your perspective that I may rejoice in Your sovereign control over all things. Thank You for hearing me and considering my petition. Let everything that I think, say, and do bring glory and honor to You. In the name of Your precious Son, Jesus Christ, I pray. Amen.

SAMPLE PRAYERS AND DEVOTIONAL EXERCISES

A Short Prayer of Repentance and Dedication

Dear Heavenly Father, I desire the fullness of Your salvation. Please forgive my sins and cleanse me from all unrighteousness. Remove everything from my life that displeases You. I reject pride, selfishness, worldliness, and evil temptation, and I embrace holiness, godliness, righteousness, and all that is good. I believe that Jesus Christ is the Son of God. I believe that He died for my sins and rose from the dead. I accept Jesus Christ as my Lord and Savior. My life is no longer my own; it belongs to Him. Thank You, Lord, for salvation and wholeness. From this day forward, I belong to You. Please continue to use my life for Your glory and honor. Amen.

An Exercise in Praise

Make a list of positive declarations about God and recite them back to Him in prayer. Some suggestions are as follows:

1. Dear God, You are wonderful. You are awesome. You are magnificent.

2. You are worthy of glory, honor, and praise. I magnify and extol You.

3. You are holy, righteous, good, loving, merciful, and kind.

4. You are all powerful, all knowing, and everywhere present.

Read a psalm of praise, such as Psalm 145, 146, 147, or 150. What do you learn about God from these Scriptures? Take a moment to think about each statement about God. If you were writing a psalm, what types of declarations would you make? Declare these things to God right now.

An Exercise in Thanksgiving

Make a list of things for which you are thankful and recite them to God in prayer. Some suggestions are as follows:

1. Dear God, I thank You for life.
2. I thank You for the loved ones You have brought into my life.
3. I thank You for food, clothing, and shelter.
4. I thank You for Jesus Christ, the Holy Spirit, and the Word of God.

Read First Thessalonians 5:16-18. Are you as thankful to God as you should be? Ask God to help you to become more thankful. At the end of this day, think about the many blessings that God brought into your life. Thank Him for these blessings.

An Acknowledgment of the Presence of the Holy Spirit

The Bible teaches us that the Holy Spirit indwells believers. Take a moment to address the indwelling Spirit within you. Ask Him to reveal Himself to you as He chooses. Invite Him to fill the empty places of your life. Wait silently in His presence for a few moments. Receive the wisdom, strength, peace, and joy that He extends to you. Thank Him for His constant help and power in all areas of the Christian life.

An Exercise in Silent Prayer

Prayer is personal communion and communication with God. Communication need not always be verbal. God can read our body language, our posture, our thoughts, our moods, everything about us. Sometimes it may be beneficial simply to come before the Lord in silence. Take 15 minutes or more to wait before the Lord in silence. Concentrate simply on being in His presence. Sometimes friends or loved ones sit together without speaking. They enjoy one another in silence. Similarly, we can spend time with God without saying much of anything. The discipline of silence gives us opportunities to focus on God before immediately making petitions. You may want to set a pen and notepad nearby to record any significant thoughts that flood your mind as you wait before the Lord. These thoughts may be Scriptures, instructions, affirmations, or other godly insights.

A Physical Exercise to Increase Awareness of God's Life

God is the source of life and well-being. Read Genesis 2:7. Take several deep breaths for about a minute. As you breathe deeply, imagine the life of God permeating your inner being. Repeat to yourself several times, "Every breath that I take is a gift from God." Read John 10:10. Take a moment to thank God for physical life, abundant life, and eternal life. Quiet yourself for a few moments and allow the life of God to strengthen and invigorate you. Welcome the healing and transformation of God's Spirit as He fills you.

An Exercise to Increase Awareness of God's Light

Read John 8:12, Ephesians 5:8-13, and First John 1:5-7. In your mind's eye, see the light of God surrounding you. Allow it to penetrate your soul. Feel its warmth and its healing effects. Ask God to illuminate every area of your life and to deliver you from the darkness of sin. Celebrate the fact that light defeats darkness. Ask the Holy Spirit to help you to walk in the light and to lead a life that is consistent with God's character. Read Matthew 5:14-16. Tell someone today about the love, mercy, and goodness of God.

A Scriptural Meditation on the Defeat of Satan and Demons

Read Colossians 2:15. Jesus Christ defeated satan, marched him naked through the streets (the imagery evoked by the verse), and rescued us from ultimate destruction. Christ disarmed, humiliated, and stripped the inimical spiritual forces opposing Him and His people, and He will ultimately cast them into the lake of fire. Although Christ has not yet destroyed these evil forces, He has curbed their authority over the children of God. Take a moment to envision satan and his demons in chains of defeat. View them trembling before the presence of Jesus Christ, even at the mention of His name. Picture yourself in a victory march with Jesus Christ. Take a moment to thank Him for securing victory over the forces of evil on your behalf.

An Exercise to Release Bitterness, Unforgiveness, and Other Negative Emotions

Take a moment to invite the Holy Spirit to control the prayer time. Ask Him to apply the full benefit of the work of Christ to your life and to infuse you with love, joy, peace, patience, and other spiritual fruit. Express to God your willingness to receive healing of bitterness, unforgiveness, and other negative emotions. Be honest with yourself and with God. Tell God how you were hurt and how you feel. Be explicit in the description of your experiences. You may want to address the offender as if he or she physically were present.

After you have talked about your feelings with God, allow the reality of His presence to comfort you. Try to imagine the Lord's response to the hurtful event that you experienced. What does He do? What does He say to you? What does He require of you? Commit yourself to obeying the Lord's instructions. Ask Him to help you to forgive those who have hurt you. Also, strengthen your resolve to give your negative emotions to Him so that He can dispose of them. Make a positive declaration such as "I choose to walk in forgiveness," "I send bitterness to the cross," or "Negativity will not be my master." Spend some time praising God and thanking Him for His goodness. If you have experienced great trauma in your past, then you may require extra help to process your feelings and emotions. There is no shame in seeking Christian counselors and other professionals to help you. God uses various means to heal our brokenness.

Placing Yourself in the Biblical Story or Passage

Sometimes it is helpful to imagine yourself as a participant in the biblical story or passage. Read the passage three times. Read it normally, read it slowly, and read it aloud. If the passage is a narrative, such as the story of the woman with the issue of blood or Blind Bartimaeus, try to imagine yourself as the main character or as another participant in the story. What is happening around you? How do you feel as a participant in this story? What transforming activities does the text cause to happen in your life? If the passage is not a story, how does it challenge your thinking or behavior? What lifestyle changes will you make because of the instructions in the text? By placing yourself in the world of the text, you personalize its message to you. As a result, you can more readily receive forgiveness, healing, deliverance, freedom, etc. God cares for you, just as He cared for the people in the Bible. Allow the truth of the Word of God to draw you into the world of the text.

Intercessory Prayer

Make a list of your family, friends, and neighbors who need prayer. Pray for their needs. Ask God to save the lost, to heal the sick, to provide financial blessings, etc. Pray for wisdom and guidance for our national leaders. Pray for church leaders and other people in authority. Pray for Christians around the world because these are your brothers and sisters in Christ.

Other Prayer and Devotional Ideas

1. Write God a poem or song or draw Him a picture.

2. If you operate in the gift of tongues, spend time each day in this spiritual exercise.

3. Design a personal spiritual retreat to spend extended time with God. You can pray, read Scripture, sing worship songs, record insights in a prayer journal, etc. Be creative.

4. Meditate (i.e., reflect) on the following Scriptures: Matthew 7:7-11 (Prayer); Matthew 18:23-35 (Forgiveness); Romans 8:31-39 (God's Love); Second Corinthians 5:17-21 (New Creation); Colossians 1:15-20 (Lordship of Jesus Christ); Hebrews 4:14-16 (Compassion of Jesus); First John 1:5-9 (Confession of Sin). Choose your own Scriptures and reflect on the truths contained in them.

CHAPTER SUMMARY

1. Prayer is personal communion and communication with God.

2. Through prayer, we fellowship with God and He grants us the wisdom and power to face the various challenges of life.

3. The fundamental requirement of effective prayer is to pray according to the will of God.

4. Discerning the will of God requires the careful study of His Word and a single-minded commitment to Him.

5. God speaks to us from the Scriptures, through wise counsel, through divine peace, through His character, and through prophecies, dreams, visions, or spiritual gifts. God has many creative ways to communicate His intentions to us.

6. The Holy Spirit helps us to pray effectively. We need to yield to His leading during prayer.

Reflection/Discussion Questions

1. What new insights did you receive from reading this chapter?

2. Do you now have a greater appreciation for the discipline of prayer?

3. Did you receive any answers to your prayers after reading this chapter and applying some of its principles?

4. What situations will you now bring before the Lord in prayer? Are you confident that He will hear you?

PRACTICAL APPLICATIONS AND ACTIVITIES

1. Tell a family member or friend about what you learned in this chapter.

2. Create your own prayer exercise. What new appreciation for God or His Word does it give you?

3. Find an opportunity this week to pray for someone who needs physical healing. Hold the person's hand or put your hand gently on the person's forehead. Pray a simple prayer for healing, such as the following: "Father, I ask You by the authority of Jesus Christ to surround this person with Your love and to release Your healing power into his or her body. I do recognize that You are greater than sickness and disease, and that Your highest plan for him/her is wholeness. We welcome the salvation, healing, and wholeness that You now extend to him/her. Amen." Were there any discernible physical or emotional results? If so, what were the results? Keep praying. God honors persistence.

Chapter 9

Wholeness Through Daily Routines and Wise Practices

Trust in the Lord with all your heart,
And lean not on your own understanding;
In all your ways acknowledge Him,
And He shall direct your paths.

—Proverbs 3:5-6 (NKJV)

A Day in the Life of a Successful Christian

Sometimes the journey toward personal wholeness involves hard work. How do we position ourselves to receive the blessings that God desires to bring into our lives? What do we do first? Is there a key to success in the Christian life? I honestly wish that I could give you a formula or recipe that would guarantee your personal success in life; however, your individual pathway to wholeness will only become clear as you walk with God on a daily, moment-by-moment basis and discipline yourself to make sound choices as He directs you. The Bible promises us in various places that God grants wisdom to His children, that He orders our steps, that He gives us the everyday resources needed to live and to survive, and that He protects us from harm and destruction. Therefore, we must learn to appropriate God's provisions for ourselves.

The Bible teaches that God extends salvation to humanity by grace through faith. Although we do not deserve God's favor, we can receive eternal life and the blessings of God through faith in Jesus Christ. Faith in the Son of God and His redemptive work on the cross is the only requirement for entry into Heaven; however, the Lord expects us to seek Him with diligence, to obey His commandments without fail, and to lead lives that coincide with the principles found in His Word. From a practical perspective, the Christian walk involves regular, consistent application of biblical truth with the help of the Holy Spirit. When we adjust our thinking and our actions to the Word of God, good success is the result (see Josh. 1:8). Someone has said that success comes from making one correct choice after another. Your journey toward personal wholeness may be a complex one or it may be simple. In either case, the journey begins with a single step in the right direction. If you will concentrate on taking simple steps in the direction of your personal goals, then you eventually will reach your destination successfully.

This chapter will highlight some of the daily and other regular routines that you will need in order to continue toward your goal of personal success and individual wholeness. You probably will be able to come up with many other practices and principles that fit your life. What is important is that you start to develop the habit of making right choices. Each day, you actively should seek to make good choices, and as God grants you wisdom, make even better choices. Mistakes will be inevitable, but you should never allow them to hinder you from realizing your potential. The appropriate response to a mistake is to learn from it, correct it, and move forward. God is an ever-present help in times of trouble. Run to Him for help with your mistakes and during your times of weakness and trouble. Do not allow your past to poison your present or prevent you from enjoying a bright future.

Every Christian should begin each day with prayer and Bible reading. I recommend that you find a quiet place with no distractions where you can meet with the Lord each day at the same time. I usually plan my morning appointments with God for at least 30 minutes. If fellowship with the Lord is important to you, then you will be eager to meet with Him and converse with Him on a consistent basis. Some of you will choose to read several chapters of the Bible per day. Others of you will follow the short reflections in yearly devotionals such as *The Word for the Day*[1] or *My Utmost for His Highest*[2]. Still others of you will prefer to have an extended time of prayer, Bible reading, singing, or other forms of worship activities. These times may require you to wake up an hour earlier, but what better way is there to spend your time than with the Creator of the universe?

I personally keep a prayer journal in which to record all types of things. For example, I write down significant events, dreams and visions, prayer requests, answers to prayers, important spiritual insights, daily Bible readings, poetry, and songs in my journal. Typically, whenever I learn something new about God or I discern His wisdom in a particularly clear way, I will include an entry of the experience in the journal. As I mentioned in the preface, the outline for the present book resulted from a process of journalizing. Many of my teachings and sermons also emerge from the process of writing in my journal. A journal keeps me accountable to my spiritual commitments and provides a written record of what God says and does in my life. I highly recommend the discipline of journalizing.

After you spend time with the Lord in listening prayer, it is necessary to use any wisdom that He gives you to plan your day. What do you feel are the general instructions that God is giving to you? God will always move you in the direction of your purpose and calling. You should nurture and utilize the spiritual gifts that He has given to you and move away from tasks and activities to which God has not called you. Often, during listening prayer, God will lead you to discontinue harmful practices, to sever unbeneficial relationships, or to bring closure to the things in your life that are fruitless and unproductive. For example, God may direct you to stop wasteful spending, avoid debt, and manage your assets more responsibly (see Prov. 21:17; 22:7; 27:23-24).

I encourage you to schedule and prioritize each day (or longer periods) so that you will not waste valuable time. What major things must you accomplish in a given day? You should devote the most energy to those items that are most important. Everyone should have short- and long-range goals. Goals should be specific, measurable, attainable, realistic, and timely (or S.M.A.R.T.).[3] Where do you want to be in six months, a year, five years, or ten years? What type of success do you envision for your future? What do you need to do right now to accomplish your goals? Do you need to enroll in a class? Do you need to save a certain amount of money each week? Do you need to talk to someone who has already succeeded in your field of interest? Whatever you can do today toward the realization of your dreams, do it! A journal is a good place to record short- and long-range goals and any progress that you make toward these goals. A wall calendar or personal organizer will help you with time management. Life will always present roadblocks and challenges to the fulfillment of your destiny; however, you must never allow what is important to you to leave your focus or slip through your fingers. Few things that are worthwhile in life come easily.

As you go about your day, take short pauses in order to reflect upon your progress. Have regular conversations with God and with yourself. Ask God to give you wisdom and to order your steps in each decision. Ask yourself whether your motives and actions are pleasing to God. Are there ways in which you could have handled a specific situation any better? Is the path you are taking leading you to a helpful, desirable, holy, or constructive outcome? You need to make a conscious decision each day to do something positive.

Slow down! Remove unnecessary haste from your life. Take time to think and to pray before you act. Instead of hurrying, you should try being consistent. Aesop's fable of the hare and the tortoise teaches us this lesson: "Slow and steady wins the race." Work regularly and diligently on projects without procrastination. Even if you only can commit a few minutes to important tasks in a given day, it is better to do so than to put off the tasks entirely until the last minute. When you become tired, take time to rest and relax, and then resume the projects. You also should actively pursue God's strength to sustain you in the completion of important tasks. Sometimes we forget to include God in our daily routines. This omission is a serious mistake. If we will include God in every area of our lives, we will find that He is more than willing to direct us (see Prov. 3:5-6).

Several years ago during a particularly stressful time at my job in the aerospace-defense industry, I needed to develop a battery of statistical tests to support several technical projects. The mathematical analysis was an integral part of validating the accuracy of a computer simulation produced by the company's team of engineers and scientists. For several days, I approached the problem in various ways; however, I failed to come up with a sufficient line of attack for the validation of the simulation. After about a week of frustration, during a lunch break, I decided to take a walk around the campus and pray for wisdom. As I walked and quieted myself before the Lord, He revealed to me in a vision a statistical technique that I had not previously learned. I returned to my office and adapted the technique to my efforts. The results were beautiful. Later that year, my team received a nomination for the highest award in the company, and I received a 23 percent raise. God will order our steps daily as we seek Him and wait patiently for His guidance. Slow down and allow the Lord to minister to you!

I strongly recommend that you take time to do some kind of physical activity each day. Go jogging or swimming. Take a bicycle ride or join a health club. Do some breathing exercises. At the very least, take extended walks several times a week. Regular exercise is an excellent way to maintain weight and reduce stress. My 83-year-old grandfather loves to work in the family garden. His active lifestyle has enabled him to overcome a number of challenges to his health. I purchased an elliptical machine for my home several years ago and I love it. I operate with more energy during the day when I exercise consistently.

In addition to physical activity, you need mental stimulation. Read a novel each month, work crossword puzzles, or solve Sudoku number games. My mother and grandmother recently attended an introductory computer course together and learned about basic word processing and the Internet. I know several people in their mid-90s whose minds are as sharp as ever. They read regularly, involve themselves in politics, attend social functions, and enjoy high-quality lives. We all need to develop the habit of keeping ourselves both physically and mentally active.

I also want to encourage you to develop the habit of thinking healthy thoughts. We cannot prevent bad thoughts from entering our minds, but we do not have to take ownership of these thoughts. Instead, we should *"take captive every thought to make it obedient to Christ"* (2 Cor. 10:5). I suggest the following daily exercise to help you with this goal. First, recognize and label each unhealthy thought. Acknowledge that you are feeling negatively, and put your feelings into words. Second, arrest the unhealthy thought. Instead of fueling the thought and allowing it to grow out of control, make a conscious decision to surrender it to Christ. Third, replace the unhealthy thought with an appropriate healthy one and respond with a positive affirmation. Declare to yourself your identity in Christ and/or what you will do or accomplish in His strength. Fourth, take a practical step that reflects your embrace of the truth that you have affirmed. Finally, rehearse the new pattern of thinking and action. It may take a while for your feelings to catch up; however, good feelings follow healthy thinking.

Throughout your day, you should actively seek to filter out negativity. Do not allow negative people to monopolize your time. Do not become a dumping ground for emotional toxic waste. Avoid negative situations to the best of your ability. Of course, life will throw many negatives your way, but you must consciously avoid the negatives that are within your power to do so. Certainly, if you find yourself in abusive situations, it would be wise to locate yourself in spiritually, emotionally, or physically safe environments.

I have developed a personal mission statement, the principles of which describe my philosophy of life. I challenge you to develop a personal philosophy by which you will live. My statement, which is too long to reproduce here in its entirety, expresses my commitment to pursue an intimate relationship with the Father, through Jesus Christ, by the power of the Holy Spirit. It communicates my desire to please God in all that I think, say, and do, and my dedication to leading others into the salvation that God extends to them through Christ. My mission statement also captures my commitment to personal and professional integrity, sexual purity, fiscal responsibility, and excellence in every area of my life.

I recommend that you develop the habit of continually improving yourself on a daily basis. Take a writing course or a seminar on public speaking. Become proficient at using a personal computer. If your job offers professional development seminars or pays for continuing education, then take advantage of what is available. I plan on learning a new language and taking piano lessons in the near future.

Journalizing and developing mission statements are activities that keep us accountable to ourselves. We also need to become accountable to others. You should take positive steps to include others in your plans, pursuits, schedules, routines, and involvements. A good friend will challenge you to remain faithful to your goals and remind you of the various commitments that you have made. A spouse also can serve as an accountability partner. Accountability can be a tremendous source of strength and encouragement. It is one way in which Christians can bear one another's burdens. I also encourage you to surround yourselves with friends who will intercede for you. Find a group of people who will commit themselves to pray for you and your needs. Everyone needs a few close friends to strengthen and to encourage them, to help them during difficult times, and to be with them during good times and bad times.

In addition to having close friends, everyone needs a mentor and apprentice. Mentors are those from whom we draw wisdom, strength, and perspective. Apprentices are those to whom we impart these things. A network of friends, mentors, and apprentices keeps a person accountable and grounded and allows people to grow together. Positive relationships and human interactions go a long way in establishing individual health and well-being. In light of this truth, I think that it is essential for Christians to show kindness to others throughout the day. A smile, a kind word, or a thoughtful action often can rescue a person from depression or other negative emotions. I sometimes have gained great satisfaction from helping someone in need or simply sharing my faith with him or her. When we sow seeds of goodness into the lives of others, we will reap a harvest of goodness in our lives as well.

Do not take your health for granted. Listen to what your body is telling you, and pay attention to any warning signs that it gives you. My aunt who is a nurse always says, "If you are good to your body, then your body will be good to you." In addition to getting physical and mental exercise, you should also eat properly every day. Avoid overindulgence in fast foods, sweets, fats, etc. Eat an apple or some grapes instead of grabbing a candy bar. Drink plenty of water throughout the day and minimize the excessive consumption of coffee, sodas, and sugary liquids. Pursue moderation in your diet, and seek God's help in controlling your cravings for food. Please stop smoking! I also advise you to get regular physicals and to keep your appointments with doctors, dentists, and other health professionals. God has placed much great wisdom on the earth to aid us in becoming whole.

As each day ends, you should reflect on the events of that day. Did you accomplish everything that you needed to accomplish? What are some ways in which you can make the next day more productive? Did you do everything that God told you to do? Did you stop doing the things that are displeasing to Him? Before you fall asleep, you should spend time with the Lord in prayer. Evening prayer presents an excellent opportunity for thanksgiving and praise. Some people enjoy reading their Bibles before they retire for the night.

A balanced life is a peaceful and rested one. We must learn to rest in the Lord and to rest ourselves physically. Resting involves accepting our human limitations and allowing the Lord to manifest His wisdom and power in the various situations that we face. I have learned that I cannot change the world all by myself. I should be dedicated and committed to the things that God has entrusted to me, but I must remember that the universe belongs to God. I am not the Messiah. I cannot fix everyone else's problems. Some things only God can handle. There is no sense worrying about things that are out of my control. I encourage you to get the proper amount of rest on a nightly basis. In the end, your body will thank you for it.

I could say many other things about routine, health, balance, and wholeness. Regular church attendance is one routine that we all should embrace. The practice evidences discipline and commitment to worship in communal settings. Attending church also enables us to fellowship with other people. The result of such fellowship is mutual edification and growth. If you are married, then I recommend a weekly date night with your spouse. Do not take the ones you love for granted. If you do not get out much, consider spending an evening at the symphony or a day at the beach with your family. Have you ever been to a sporting event? When is the last time that you took a real vacation? Living a balanced lifestyle will aid you in your pursuit of wholeness. Take care of yourself and consistently do the things that are spiritually, emotionally, and physically healthy.

I cannot stress enough the importance of developing godly habits, good routines, and wise practices. Daniel was able to face the lion's den because he had been consistent in his walk with the Lord and dedicated to the discipline of prayer. Similarly, the three Hebrew boys were bold in facing the fiery furnace because they had learned through experience that God is faithful. Joseph consistently walked in integrity at each phase of his life and eventually became the second most powerful man in Egypt. Paul pointed to physical discipline as an aspect of his commitment to the Lord. The Lord Jesus Christ Himself had a regular prayer life, the strength from which indubitably helped Him to endure the agony of the cross. Sometimes routines may seem tedious and unproductive, but they often can prepare us to be in the right place at the right time to receive unexpected blessings from God. The man at the pool of Bethesda consistently went to the site for 38 years without success but later encountered the Great Physician. His divine appointment to receive wholeness finally arrived. Do not give up because you do not immediately see the full fruit of your actions. Your day is coming.

In Chapter 6, I told the story of my battle with high blood sugar. What I did not mention was that for a year or two preceding the dream of July 31, 2001, I would awaken each morning about 3:00 a.m. and pray beside my bed. Sometimes I would awaken several hours later and discover that I was still on my knees. On July 31, my routine of prayer had a far different result than before. The prayer time led to the dream (or vision) in which God promised to heal me. My divine encounter arrived after a period of routine. Many good things can happen to us because we follow godly routines and develop wise practices.

A Powerful Daily Habit: Putting on the Full Armor of God

There are many spiritual resources available to us because of Jesus' work of salvation. These resources prepare us for all aspects of the Christian life. In Ephesians 6:10-18, Paul encourages us to put on the full armor of God and mentions six pieces of equipment: (1) the belt of truth; (2) the breastplate of righteousness; (3) the footwear of the Gospel; (4) the shield of faith; (5) the helmet of salvation; and (6) the sword of the Spirit. The process of putting on the full armor of God should be included in your daily routine of prayer. If you will take advantage of the spiritual resources that God supplies, then your victory against evil forces will be a certainty.

The first two pieces of armor deal with our Christian character. We must put on the belt of truth and the breastplate of righteousness. When we put on the belt of truth, we commit ourselves to truthfulness in our daily living. Lying is never good. It usually leads us into a vicious cycle of deceit where we often find ourselves telling bigger and more elaborate lies to cover up the initial fabrication. The devil thrives in an atmosphere of dishonesty. Remove his access to your life by allowing truth to characterize your daily walk.

Righteousness refers to proper action or conduct. It is doing what we know is the right thing to do in every situation. By putting on God's righteousness each day, we become imitators of Him (see Eph. 5:1-2). To put on truth and righteousness is to *"put on the new self, created to be like God in true righteousness and holiness"* (Eph. 4:24). It is to follow Jesus Christ in word and deed. It is to be a person of genuineness and integrity and to separate oneself from sinful activity. Part of your protection from evil involves abstaining from the things that you know will invite evil into your life. There is divine safety in leading a life of Christian character. Doing so will enable you to stand unmoved by the enemy.

Ephesians 6:15 describes the importance of proper footwear. Our feet must be *"fitted with the readiness that comes from the gospel of peace."* The New English Bible (NEB) reads, *"Let the shoes on your feet be the gospel of peace, to give you firm footing."* Our readiness for combat and for standing firm in battle comes from the Gospel of peace. We need to hear the Gospel, to embrace the Gospel, and to lead a life that is consistent with the truth of the Gospel. Furthermore, we must never forget that the Gospel message is one of peace. The biblical concept of peace is more than a state of quietness or stillness; it also includes the notion of wholeness, completeness, and well-being. Everything that you need to be whole is in God's Word. Everything that you need to be complete is in Christ, who is the Living Word. The good news of the Gospel is that Jesus saves. He is the Prince of Peace. He is the Source of Wholeness. He is our all in all.

The fourth piece of armor is the shield of faith. Faith is complete reliance on and trust in God. Because God continues to demonstrate that He is reliable and trustworthy, we can face the challenges of each new day with the full assurance of His presence, power, and provision. A shield protects the heart. To take up the shield of faith is to believe in your heart that God will save, deliver, and protect you from the evil one. Try not to allow extended battles to discourage you, though. Remember that Christ already has won the war against evil forces. God will set everything in order when the time is right.

Verse 17 indicates that the helmet of salvation is available for the daily protection and victory of believers. The helmet of salvation is the fifth piece of armor. A helmet protects the head, the place where understanding happens. We must grow in our understanding of the many resources, provisions, and benefits of salvation. When we do, we are more likely to lead lives that reflect the victory that God intends for us to walk in on a daily basis, and we are less likely to believe the devil's lies about our position in Christ. To put on the helmet of salvation is to align your thinking with God's good intent toward you. It is to appropriate His victory over evil and its effects. It is to receive the fullness of what He provides for you through Christ. God has the power to save you, and nothing can separate you from His love.

The second piece of armor mentioned in verse 17 and the sixth overall is the sword of the Spirit. The sword of the Spirit is the Word of God. The Greek term translated as "word" here in Ephesians is *rhema*, which basically means, "a word that is spoken." The sword of Ephesians 6 is the portion of the Bible that the Holy Spirit brings to our remembrance in order for us to speak out against the deception of the evil one. The Lord Jesus Christ used the sword of the Spirit in Matthew 4 to overcome satan in the wilderness. He said in Matthew 4:4, quoting from Deuteronomy 8:3, *"Man does not live on bread alone, but on every word [rhema] that comes from the mouth of God."* Jesus' use of Scripture against the evil one is a pattern for us. We too can use Holy Spirit-empowered words of Scripture to repel demonic assault. We also can think of the spoken word or the *rhema* of God as the proclamation of the Gospel. When we proclaim the Gospel under the power of the Holy Spirit, we do serious damage to the kingdom of darkness.

How do we "put on" the armor of God in our daily lives and when do we do it? We put on the armor daily (or continually) by being men and women of character and integrity (belt and breastplate).

We must submit to God, spend time in His Word, and allow the truth of the Gospel (footwear) to prepare our hearts and minds so that we can resist the enemy in his attacks against our faith (shield) and our assurance of salvation in Christ (helmet). Finally, we remain sensitive to the Holy Spirit so that He can give us specific instructions from the Word (sword) to use against the evil one when he attacks us.

A Prayer for Putting on the Full Armor of God

Dear Heavenly Father, I come to You with an attitude of humility and confidence, and I ask You to strengthen me by the power of the Holy Spirit. By faith, I put on the full armor of God so that I can stand against the wiles and deceitfulness of the devil. Dear Lord, I put on the belt of truth, and I refuse to accept the lies of the enemy. Your Word is truth, so I will lead a life that is consistent with the Word, a life of integrity and holiness. I put on the breastplate of righteousness, knowing that it is because of the sacrifice of Jesus Christ I have been made righteous. Therefore, dear God, I will walk in righteousness and lead a life that reflects Christian character. I put on the footwear of the Gospel of peace, knowing that Jesus Christ is the Prince of Peace and the Gospel is the power of God unto salvation. I take, above all, the shield of faith, with which I can quench all the flaming arrows of the wicked one. Help me, O God, to exhibit unwavering faith and confidence in You. Help me to trust in Your character, Your power, and Your promises—no matter what circumstances I may face. I put on the helmet of salvation, rejoicing in what You have done for me, wiping away my sins, giving me eternal life, and protecting my mind from the condemnation of the enemy. Finally, Heavenly Father, I wield the sword of the Spirit, which is the spoken Word that You bring to me in each specific situation to defeat the enemy. Thank You, Father, for the divine protection of Your armor. Help me always to avail

myself of Your infinite resources. In the name of the Lord
Jesus Christ, I pray. Amen.

EXCELLENCE IN THE STUDY OF THE WORD OF GOD

I challenge you to pursue excellence in all things, especially the
study and application of God's Word. The Bible tells us in Second
Timothy 2:15:

> Be diligent to present yourself approved to God, a worker
> who does not need to be ashamed, rightly dividing the
> word of truth (NKJV).

Although this verse applies specifically to those who teach the
Word of God, it also has implications for every Christian. God
wants all of us to understand His Word. The Bible is the unique,
written Word of God containing everything that we need to enter
into a life-changing and intimate relationship with God. Second
Timothy 3:16-17 informs us:

> All Scripture is God-breathed [or inspired] and is
> useful for teaching, rebuking, correcting and training in
> righteousness, so that the man [or woman] of God may
> be thoroughly equipped for every good work.

I also appreciate the words of Psalm 119:130: "The unfolding
of Your words gives light; it gives understanding to the simple."
The Holy Spirit uses the Word of God to bring illumination and
revelation to the child of God.

Although we may desire to understand God's Word more
clearly, we will never do so until we put forth responsible effort.
Any valuable enterprise requires quality time and personal discipline. If the study of God's Word is important to us, then we will
spend time searching the Scriptures. This is why Second Timothy
2:15 requires us to pursue the discovery of truth with diligence.

We must learn to handle the Word of God with extreme care, humility, and reverence.

I cannot stress enough the importance of knowing and obeying the Word of God, especially in this modern society where false teachings and philosophies of many kinds continually bombard us. There is increasing interest in the New Age movement and in the occult, and various cults are proselytizing our young people with evangelistic fervor. Biblical maturity is so crucial. Paul states in Ephesians 4:14 that the mature saint:

> *Will no longer be* [as an infant] *tossed back and forth by the waves, and blown here and there by every wind of teaching and by the cunning and craftiness of men in their deceitful scheming.*

Therefore, the Body of Christ desperately needs good teachers as well as the other fivefold ministry offices of apostle, prophet, evangelist, and pastor.

I believe that God is calling all of us to a higher level of excellence in the study of His Word. I challenge some of you reading this book to consider attending a Bible college or seminary, taking correspondence courses, or pursuing other educational activities that will further immerse you in the Word of God. Your appreciation for God's truth will grow tremendously!

Some of you may not have the opportunity to study the Word in formal settings; however, you can still acquire tools to help you to study the Bible more effectively. All Christians need a good study Bible, a Bible dictionary or handbook, access to several modern translations, such as the New International Version or the New King James Version, a good commentary, and a concordance. Your local Christian bookstore will carry a number of these resources, along with other computerized helps. You will also find helpful Bible resources on the Internet. I suggest the following guiding principles to aid you in your Bible study times.

- Before you engage in Bible study, you should pray and ask God for wisdom and guidance (see Prov. 3:5-6). Read the introduction to the book of the Bible that you want to study.

- Read a large section of the book or the entire book if you can so that you will understand the story or passage of interest. To whom is the writer speaking? Where does the story take place? Who are the main characters in the story? What is the main issue being discussed?

- Read a short passage. Look up any words that you do not understand. Try to explain the passage in your own words.

- Read the footnotes and articles in your study Bible. Read a commentary to help you to understand any background information that is relevant to the passage.

- Discuss the passage with others, especially teachers or other knowledgeable leaders.

- You need to be aware that the Bible contains different types of literature or genres (e.g., epistles, narratives, Gospels, parables, prophecy, and wisdom literature). Some Scripture is literal. The Bible also contains parables or stories that get a single point across to the reader. Some Scripture is allegorical or symbolic. In an allegory, one object represents something else. The Book of Revelation contains a lot of symbolism.

- Bible study is a lifelong process. No matter how much we may know, there always will be more to learn.

Chapter Summary

1. Sometimes wholeness results from daily routines and wise practices.

2. The consistent application of biblical truth is necessary for personal success in life.

3. The Christian life is one of warfare against evil forces.

4. God has equipped us with spiritual armor to win the battle against powers and authorities. This armor represents the resources of our salvation that are available to us in the Christian walk.

5. The pieces of the armor include the belt of truth, breastplate of righteousness, footwear of the Gospel of peace, shield of faith, helmet of salvation, and sword of the Spirit (Word of God).

6. We put on the armor by embracing the truth of God's Word, through obedience to the Word, and through prayerful listening to the direction of the Holy Spirit.

7. The Word of God contains principles relating to every aspect of our lives. God cares about the whole person—spirit, soul, and body. He wants us to be healthy in every way.

Reflection/Discussion Questions

1. What new insights did you receive from reading this chapter?

2. What daily routines and wise practices do you now engage in?

3. What unwise routines and foolish practices do you need to discontinue?

4. How does Christian character protect us from the wiles of the devil?

5. Specifically, how do we put on the armor of God in our daily lives? When do we do it?

6. How real has the spiritual battle been to you? What types of flaming arrows has the enemy directed toward you? How did you obtain victory?

7. Do you read the Word of God on a daily basis?

8. How does the present chapter relate to the previous chapters in this book?

PRACTICAL APPLICATIONS AND ACTIVITIES

1. Begin the practice of keeping a prayer journal.

2. Tell a family member or friend about what you learned in this chapter.

3. With the moral support of a friend or a spouse, eat healthily and get some exercise for the next three days. How do you feel?

4. Read the Book of Ephesians and record the occurrences of "in Christ," "by Christ," "in Him," "through Him," and other similar phrases. What do these phrases reveal about the blessings and privileges that God gives to believers?

5. Read Psalm 119. Record in a journal everything that the psalm reveals about the Word of God. This exercise may take you a few days to complete.

6. Teach someone this week how to put on spiritual armor.

7. Find an opportunity this week to schedule your Bible reading for the next seven days.

CHAPTER 10

Ministering Wholeness to Broken Individuals: A Case Study

Carry each other's burdens, and in this way you will fulfill the law of Christ.

—Galatians 6:2

Be alert and always keep on praying for all the saints.

—Ephesians 6:18b

SUSAN N. PAYNE: A WOMAN IN TURMOIL

Sometimes God causes us to encounter hurting people so that He can use us to minister to the broken areas of their lives. In these instances, we become God's agents of salvation, healing, and blessing. We become His ambassadors who represent the good news of Jesus Christ to a dying world. We may feel inadequate at times to handle the challenges of ministry to others; however, God often uses ordinary people to do extraordinary things. Moses had a speech impediment; Esther was an adoptee; Amos was a herdsman; and Mary was a young woman of humble beginnings. God used each of them in a very special way. Even though we all have weaknesses and broken areas ourselves, we are not excused from serving God. When we make ourselves available to Him, He will empower us to do every assignment that He gives us.

The following letter is from an imaginary individual named Susan N. Payne who is suffering from several spiritual, emotional, and physical problems. She needs to experience wholeness in her life, and she is reaching out to you for help. Are you ready for the challenge? Can you share with Ms. Payne some biblical principles to help her during this time of distress? In this chapter, we will explore various issues involved in ministry to Susan N. Payne. It is not the goal of this chapter to create a formula for ministry that will work in every case, but rather to get you thinking about how God's Word applies to the human condition. This chapter will reinforce much of the material from earlier chapters in the book and should give you some ways to approach sensitive situations like Susan's with care and thoughtfulness. Let us now examine the desperate cry for help from Susan N. Payne.

Susan's Letter of Distress

December 21, 2010

Dear Saint of God,

My name is Susan N. Payne, and I seriously need your prayers. I am going through a real crisis right now, and I am terrified. I sometimes wonder if God has forgotten me. I am only 35 years old, and I am suffering from severe arthritis in my wrists, high blood pressure, and a serious heart condition. I suspect that my neighbor, who is involved in the occult, is casting a spell on me. We used to experiment with Ouija boards, tarot cards, and white witchcraft until I became a Christian three years ago.

In addition, my kids are unruly. They tell me that they do not want anything to do with God anymore, and if God really loved them, He would not have taken their dad in a skiing accident last year. My kids are not bad kids; they are just discouraged. Although I have not really admitted this to anyone, I myself have been quite upset with God for taking my husband. My husband and I had an argument before the accident and never had the chance to patch things up. He really hurt me, but I am glad that he received salvation a year ago.

I believe that God will heal my afflictions because of what Isaiah 53:5 and First Peter 2:24 say about physical healing. I think that I will stop taking medication and simply claim my healing by faith. God needs to do something quick—I feel like I am losing my mind! My address and phone number are included below.

Sincerely,

Susan N. Payne

PRELIMINARY CONSIDERATIONS

The very first thing that you should do before responding to Susan's situation is to read the letter thoughtfully and prayerfully. You need to understand what Susan is attempting to communicate through her correspondence. What are her needs? Is she coherent? Is she in immediate danger? Are her children in immediate danger? Notice the date of the letter. It is a strong possibility that Susan is overly depressed because of the impending holiday season. At the very least, you will need to extend some kindness and understanding to her. Ask God to give you a heart of compassion toward Susan so that you will be able to minister effectively to her. You also may want to bring in another mature believer to help you to pray for her.

It is definitely unwise to discontinue medication without a doctor's approval. Faith in God does not require us to make foolish or presumptuous decisions or to put ourselves at risk. It will be necessary to encourage Susan to follow the advice of her physician. If Susan has concerns about her doctor, she should seek secondary medical opinions; however, God has a sensible plan for Susan to follow. He has a viable pathway to her individual wholeness. Jesus Christ Himself said that the sick need a physician (see Matt. 9:12). You should find a loving way to communicate the Savior's declaration to Susan.

Susan's Letter From a Biblical Perspective

After you have read Susan's letter thoughtfully and prayerfully, you should make a list of her needs and concerns, and what the Bible says about each of them. For example, Susan says, "I am going through a real crisis...and I am terrified." Therefore, she needs wisdom, peace, and freedom from fear. Three Scriptures that relate to these are James 1:5, Philippians 4:6-7, and Psalm 34:4. Susan also says, "I sometimes wonder if God has forgotten me." She needs reassurance that God is with her (see Ps. 23:4; 46:1; Heb. 13:5). Below are several statements in Susan's letter followed by sample scriptural considerations.

- "I suspect that my neighbor, who is involved in the occult, is casting a spell on me" (see Col. 2:15; Isa. 54:17).

- "We used to experiment with Ouija boards, tarot cards, and white witchcraft until I became a Christian three years ago" (see James 4:7).

- "In addition, my kids are unruly. They tell me that they do not want anything to do with God anymore, and if God really loved them, He would not have taken their dad in a skiing accident last year...I myself have been quite upset with God for taking my husband" (see Ps. 116:15; Rom. 8:35-39; 1 Cor. 15:51-58; 2 Cor. 1:3-4; Rev. 21:4).

- "My husband and I had an argument before the accident and never had the chance to patch things up. He really hurt me..." (see Matt. 6:5-15; Mark 11:22-26).

The purpose of gathering scriptural insights is not "Bible thumping" or "beating Susan over the head." The purpose of gathering Scriptures is to gain a godly perspective on what Susan is experiencing.

Susan's Needs in Light of the Chapters in This Book

1. Susan needs to know that God is the source of her life, security, and well-being. Furthermore, He is an ever-present help in times of trouble. Susan can trust Him during this time of grief, turmoil, and physical trial. God desires a personal relationship with her and seeks to give her abundant life through Jesus Christ.

2. Jesus Christ is the Savior. He wants to rescue Susan from the things that diminish or destroy her in her spirit, mind, body, relationships, and other aspects of her humanity. The Lord's heart is full of compassion for Susan, so she can reach out to Him in faith.

3. Susan benefits from the Savior's life, death, burial, resurrection, and ascension. She can rest in the Lord's completed work of salvation.

4. The Lord can cleanse Susan of the sins of her past, and He can rescue her from current satanic deception and influence.

5. As a child of God, Susan also can cast her care on Him and receive His peace and joy.

6. Jesus Christ can heal Susan of physical infirmities through spiritual gifts.

7. Christ also can work miracles on Susan's behalf. No challenge is too great, and no issue is too late for the miracle-working Christ.

8. The wisdom and power of God are available to Susan through prayer.

9. Susan also can play a part in her own process of healing by engaging in wise practices. She definitely should continue to take her medicine.

A Prayer for Susan

Before you contact Susan, you should spend time in prayer. There is no single correct way to pray for her. Even a prayer such as, "Dear God, please help Susan by Your gracious power," can be effective; however, I suggest a prayer similar to the following:

Dear Heavenly Father, I begin this prayer in an attitude of reverence and thankfulness, honoring You for who You are and for what You have done, especially in the sending of Your Son, Jesus Christ. Thank You, Jesus, for the tremendous work that You did on the cross, securing human redemption and defeating every principality and power. Thank You for the precious Holy Spirit who indwells Your people and transforms them into Your image. Please grant me wisdom in this time of prayer to know Your will and to act according to Your direction. If there is anything in my heart that is displeasing in Your sight, I pray for Your forgiveness and for the cleansing power of the blood of Jesus to purify my heart.

Lord, I humble myself before You, but I also approach You in full confidence, knowing that whatever I ask for that is according to Your will is going to manifest in Your timing. I know that You are a good God, meaning that You are the source of all that makes life possible and meaningful. As such, You have the best interests of Your people at heart. Specifically, then, I would like to uplift Your child Susan before You. I pray that You would comfort her and her family in their time of suffering.

Give them peace that surpasses human understanding and demonstrate to them that You are a God of incomparable mercy, grace, and generosity.

I pray that You will give Susan wisdom concerning her decision to cease medical treatments. I pray that You will reveal Yourself clearly and powerfully to Susan and to her children so that they will know that You love them and that You are present in their situation. Father, bring healing where healing is needed; bring deliverance where deliverance is needed; and bring strength where strength is needed. Work this entire situation out for good as You have promised in Your Word....As I speak to Susan, please help me to minister with the love, wisdom, and heart of the Savior. Amen.

Ministering to Susan Face to Face

If Susan lives far away, you may need to minister to her on the phone or recommend her to a nearby ministry. If she is local, then you should arrange a face-to-face meeting. It would be a good idea to go with another mature Christian friend or minister. One of you should be female. As you prepare to meet with Susan, remember that God is the one who heals. It is not your responsibility to solve all of Susan's problems. You are only an agent of God's love and power. In addition, you should not give Susan any medical or psychological instruction unless you are a trained professional in these areas. Also, remember that Susan is a real person and not simply an object of ministry. Be prepared to listen to her and to show her love and understanding.

When you eventually talk to Susan, allow her to express herself as completely as possible. Silently ask the Holy Spirit for any instructions while Susan is speaking. After Susan has spoken, reassure her of God's presence and concern. Share any comforting

Scriptures that God brings to mind. After reassuring Susan of God's presence, love, compassion, sympathy, etc., it probably would be a good idea to discourage her from discontinuing her medicine. The Bible never condemns medicine, and God often uses doctors to help us to become well. Although it is certainly true that Christ secured healing for humanity through the cross, we will not experience the complete eradication of sickness and death until His return. In the meantime, there is no shame in utilizing whatever provisions God has placed on the earth.[1]

After you have talked a while with Susan, you should lead her in prayer. Ask the Holy Spirit for wisdom and follow His steps. Be open to the manifestation of spiritual gifts. The Lord may reveal, for example, that He desires to bring physical healing to her supernaturally through your prayers. Even if this is the case, though, Susan should confirm her condition with her doctor.

Susan definitely needs to know that Christ defeated satan at Calvary, that there is healing in forgiveness, and that God is on her side. You should encourage her to become active in church and to get her children involved in a vibrant youth ministry. Susan's improved outlook will most certainly affect her children. Susan and her children also would probably benefit from some grief counseling. As you minister to Susan, trust the Holy Spirit to lead you in specific directions. You should allow Susan herself to pray as she receives the courage to do so. Ask her what she believes the Lord is saying to her.

A number of final considerations may be helpful to Susan. Susan would benefit from a compilation of comforting Scriptures. Express to Susan the necessity of fellowship with other believers in church, support groups, etc. Arrange for someone to check in with her on a periodic basis. Certainly, you should pray for her regularly. I believe that she is going to be OK.

Chapter Summary

1. Sometimes God uses His people to minister wholeness to others.

2. Ministry to hurting people requires wisdom, compassion, and sensitivity.

REFLECTION/DISCUSSION QUESTIONS

1. What new insights did you receive from reading this chapter?

2. Have you ever encountered anyone with problems similar to those of Susan? How did you minister to the person?

3. Do you feel better equipped to deal with sensitive situations after reading this chapter?

4. What advice would you give Susan that we did not mention in this chapter?

Practical Applications and Activities

1. Pray for someone in need this week.

2. Tell a family member or friend about what you learned in this chapter.

3. Ask God each day to give you divinely appointed opportunities to manifest His love, mercy, grace, compassion, and power to others.

Conclusion

In this book, I have attempted to establish that salvation involves more than the believer's entry into Heaven. Salvation includes the totality of God's remedy for sin and its effects throughout human history. Sin separates us from God and leads to brokenness in all areas of life. Because of sin, creation suffers from deterioration, futility, and decomposition. Human beings face illnesses, pain, and death because of the problem of sin.

Yet, there is good news for humankind. God dealt with the sin problem by sending His Son, Jesus Christ, to earth. Jesus conquered sin, sickness, satan, and death through His redemptive work on the cross and through His resurrection. The Lord now enables us to experience eternal life through faith in Him. Eternal life begins in the present and will continue into the future. Salvation, then, is God's continual rescue of humanity from the things that diminish or destroy us in our spirits, souls, bodies, relationships, and other areas of our humanity. God will continue to restore this broken world until the day when the old order of things has passed away.

Sometimes the pain, chaos, evil, and disorder in the world may discourage us; however, we can derive encouragement from the reality that God loves us and that He is in control. We must trust Him although we cannot see everything that He is doing. God gave us the greatest gift in the universe, His Son, Jesus Christ, and if God gave us Christ, He will give us anything else that we need.

Jesus Christ is the Savior. He delivers us from evil. All natural disasters, physical infirmities, mental illnesses, emotional bondages, demonic entities, and other destructive realities ultimately find their defeat with the Lord Jesus Christ. In the Savior's ministry on earth, He continually worked to bring wholeness to hurting individuals. His ministry was one of love, authority, power, and compassion.

When Jesus returned to Heaven, He sent the Holy Spirit to empower the Church to continue His ministry until the Second Coming. The Church as the Body of Christ participates with God to advance His Kingdom on earth. The Church proclaims the good news that Jesus saves, heals, delivers, restores, blesses, etc. Available to the Church are various spiritual gifts that confirm her message and make her more effective in serving people. Gifts of healings, for example, manifest the love of God and reveal His power to restore broken bodies, souls, and spirits.

We can do a number of things to appropriate God's provisions for our individual wholeness. We must pursue God with expectation and trust. We also must live holy and consciously do the things of which God approves. It is imperative that we engage in practices that we know to be spiritually, emotionally, and physically healthy. God does not perform miracles in order to exempt us from living wisely.

Those who desire wholeness in their lives will have to become students of the Word, individuals of prayer, and people of discipline. The Bible contains the general wisdom that God wants us to apply to our lives. Prayer is the way in which we communicate with God to receive His specific directions. Discipline will ensure that we put in the necessary effort to succeed in our journey toward wholeness. Anything worthwhile requires investment and sacrifice on our part. Wholeness involves a process of hearing God, utilizing His resources, and obeying His commands. I pray that you will experience all that God has for you.

Endnotes

Preface

1. Although a sin can refer to an individual act of wrongdoing, sin more generally defined is a state of alienation or separation from God.

Chapter I

1. Jonathan Edwards, *The Nature of True Virtue* (Boston, 1765), 126.

2. The reader who is new to theology (i.e., the study of God) may wish to consult a basic introduction to the discipline. A wealth of theological helps can be found online or at your local Christian bookstore.

3. The Nicene Creed (A.D. 325), an early Christian statement of faith, declared that Christ is "of the same substance (*homoousios*) as the Father." The English word *consubstantial* captures the meaning of the Greek *homoousios*.

4. The word *Trinity* simply means "tri-unity" or "three-in-one."

5. *Person* is the Greek *hypostasis* in early Christian confessions. Hence, God is one *ousia* (substance), yet three *hypostases* (persons).

6. Redemption refers to a release from prison or slavery through the payment of a ransom. Jesus Christ redeems us from the bondage of sin. The price paid to secure our redemption was His shed blood on the cross.

7. God's *shalom* (peace) is more than quietness or stillness. It also means completeness, wholeness, and well-being. God wants to make us whole. He wants to bring salvation to the broken areas of our lives.

8. Even though we all will die someday, the resurrection of Jesus Christ assures us that death has no final victory over believers (e.g., see 1 Cor. 6:14; 2 Cor. 4:14; and 1 Cor. 15:12-28).

9. The compound name *Yahweh-rohi* means, "The Lord is my shepherd." David's designation of the Lord reminds us that we too can personalize whatever the Lord reveals about Himself (e.g., "The Lord is *my* healer" or "The Lord is *my* peace").

Chapter 2

1. Francis MacNutt, *Healing* (Altamonte Springs, FL: Creation House, 1995; originally published, 1988), 75, 96.

2. See Francis MacNutt, *Healing*, Chapter 3.

3. The Old Testament also links salvation and healing. See, for example, Psalm 103:2-3.

4. This is the thesis of Howard M. Ervin, *Healing: Sign of the Kingdom* (Peabody, MA: Hendrickson, 2002), 1, 23.

5. Charles Wesley, "Love Divine, All Loves Excelling" (1747), *The United Methodist Hymnal* (Nashville: UMPH, 1989), hymn #384.

6. See William L. Lane, *The Gospel of Mark*, The New International Commentary on the New Testament (Grand Rapids, MI: Eerdmans, 1974), 192, note 46.

7. Thomas à Kempis, *The Imitation of Christ*, Book III, Chapter 1; translated by Aloysius Croft and Harold Bolton (Milwaukee: The Bruce Publishing Company, 1940), 84.

8. Helen H. Lemmel, "Turn Your Eyes upon Jesus" (London, 1922).

9. John Wimber, "Spirit Song" (Mercy/Vineyard Publishing, 1979).

CHAPTER 3

1. George Bennard, "The Old Rugged Cross" (1913).

2. The word *passion* speaks of powerful and intense emotion. Although we now commonly associate the term with strong romantic feelings, the word in its original Latin sense refers to suffering and agony. The passion narrative is found in Matthew 26–27, Mark 14–15, and Luke 22-23. The narrative in John's Gospel is found throughout chapters 10 through 19.

3. In First Corinthians 11:17-34, Paul is particularly sensitive to disgraceful conduct and attitudes that foster disorder and disunity among the people of God. For example, some within the Corinthian community were overeating and drinking excessively during the solemn celebration of the Lord's Supper. Paul warns that these and other sins must be confessed and abandoned out of love for others and respect for Christ's sacrifice. Not to do so is to invite judgment, possibly sickness or death, into one's life.

4. Glendolyn K. Graves, "The Blood Has Already Been Shed" (1988). Used by permission.

5. Robert Lowry, "Nothing but the Blood" (New York: Biglow & Main, 1876).

6. We can increase the manifestation of the Holy Spirit's power in our lives through earnest prayer (see Luke 11:9-13), through the avoidance of sin (see Eph. 4:25-32), through the cultivation of a lifestyle of worship (see Eph. 5:18-20), through the exercise of faith and expectation (see Acts 4:23-31), and through walking in love (see 1 Cor. 13; Gal. 5:22-23). We stir up spiritual gifts by actively using what God has placed within us (see 2 Tim. 1:6).

Chapter 4

1. John R.W. Stott, *The Letters of John*, Tyndale New Testament Commentaries (Grand Rapids, MI: William B. Eerdmans Publishing Company, 1998), 194.

2. When we fail to walk in obedience to God, we open ourselves up to tremendous pain and brokenness. Failure to follow godly standards of sexuality, for example, leads to many unplanned pregnancies and sexually transmitted diseases (STDs). I recently read a statistic that indicated that there are around 19 million new cases of STDs per year in the United States, almost half of which occur among young people between the ages of 15 to 24. These STDs come at an estimated healthcare cost of $13 billion per year. See Centers for Disease Control and Prevention (CDC), *Trends in Reportable Sexually Transmitted Diseases in the United States*, 2004.

3. John Newton, *Olney Hymns* (London: W. Oliver, 1779).

4. The English word *poem* comes from the Greek word *poiema.*

5. Here I paraphrase the French Reformer John Calvin, who stated, "Faith alone justifies, but the faith which justifies is not alone." See W.H. Griffith Thomas, *The Principles of Theology* (London: Church Book Room Press, 1963), 61.

Justification is the aspect of salvation through which God puts us into right relationship with Himself. "To justify" is a legal term meaning "to declare righteous."

6. For some of the technical information in this and the next section, I am indebted to the following commentaries: F.F. Bruce, *The Epistles to the Colossians, to Philemon, and to the Ephesians*, The New International Commentary on the New Testament, ed. F.F. Bruce (Grand Rapids, MI: William B. Eerdmans Publishing Company, 1984); Francis Foulkes, *Ephesians*, Tyndale New Testament Commentaries (Grand Rapids, MI: William B. Eerdmans Publishing Company, 1989); Peter T. O'Brien, *The Letter to the Ephesians*, The Pillar New Testament Commentary, ed. D.A. Carson (Grand Rapids, MI: William B. Eerdmans Publishing Company, 1999); and Arthur G. Patzia, *Ephesians, Colossians, Philemon*, New International Biblical Commentary (Peabody, MA: Hendrickson Publishers, 1990).

7. Paul's call for inward renewal in Ephesians 4:23 is similar to his exhortation in Romans 12:2: *"Be transformed by the renewing of your mind."*

8. See Bruce, *Ephesians*, 360 and Patzia, *Ephesians*, 252.

9. Paul's exhortation in verse 26 is an allusion to Psalm 4:4, which states, *"In your anger do not sin; when you are on your beds, search your hearts and be silent."*

10. Patzia, *Ephesians*, 253.

11. Foulkes, *Ephesians*, 143.

12. See Bruce, *Ephesians*, 363 and Patzia, *Ephesians*, 253-4.

13. See the discussion of sexual immorality, impurity, and greed in Patzia, *Ephesians*, 257.

14. I recommend a number of resources to break the stronghold of pornography. See, in particular, Stephen Arterburn, Fred Stoeker, and Mike Yorkey, *Every Man's Battle* (Colorado Springs, CO: WaterBrook Press, 2000) and Signa Bodish-baugh, *Illusions of Intimacy: Unmasking Patterns of Sexual Addiction and Bringing Deep Healing to Those Who Struggle* (Tonbridge, England: Sovereign World, 2004). For a helpful discussion of pornography addiction from the perspective of a neuroscientist, see William M. Struthers, *Wired for Intimacy: How Pornography Hijacks the Male Brain* (Downers Grove, IL: InterVarsity Press, 2009). I also recommend Tom Davis and Tammy Maltby, *Confessions of a Good Christian Guy* (Nashville, TN: Thomas Nelson, 2007), chapter 2. This recent book deals with a number of issues in addition to pornography related to brokenness in males. Women will receive great benefit from Shannon Ethridge, *Every Woman's Battle: Discovering God's Plan for Sexual and Emotional Fulfillment* (Colorado Springs, CO: WaterBrook Press, 2003). Several Internet courses related to sexual purity and spiritual growth are located online at http://www.settingcaptivesfree.com.

15. Masturbation is almost a universal part of self-discovery, especially for teenage boys. The practice, however, is immature. As a person develops a healthy social life and begins to interact with real people in godly ways, his or her preoccupation with selfish sexuality should diminish. Although it is doubtful that a single act of masturbation will lead to eternal damnation, there is no doubt that compulsive masturbation, especially with the use of pornography, is sinful.

16. Particularly helpful for the definitions in this paragraph were Foulkes, *Ephesians*, 149-50; O'Brien, *Ephesians*, 360-1; and Patzia, *Ephesians*, 257.

17. Judson W. Van de Venter, "I Surrender All" (1896).

18. For an excellent book on the importance and benefits of fasting, see Elmer L. Towns, *Fasting for Spiritual Breakthrough* (Ventura, CA: Regal Books/Gospel Light Publishers, 1996). In this immensely practical book, Towns discusses several types of fasts and how fasting can aid persons in their search for guidance, spiritual renewal, freedom from sinful practices, physical healing, emotional well-being, etc.

19. See Neil T. Anderson, *The Bondage Breaker*, new edition (Eugene, OR: Harvest House Publishers, 2006) and Ed Murphy, *The Handbook of Spiritual Warfare* (Nashville, TN: Thomas Nelson, 1992). See also Francis MacNutt, *Deliverance from Evil Spirits: A Practical Manual* (Grand Rapids, MI: Chosen Books, 2009; originally published, 1995).

20. *New International Reader's Version* (Grand Rapids, MI: Zondervan, 1998).

CHAPTER 5

1. Quoted in Frank S. Mead, ed., *12,000 Religious Quotations* (Grand Rapids, MI: Baker Book House, 1989; originally published: Judy D. Mead, *The Encyclopedia of Religious Quotations*, 1965), 477.

2. Emily Dickinson, "Not in Vain," in Roy J. Cook, compiler, *One Hundred and One Famous Poems* (Chicago: Contemporary Books, Inc., 1958), 30.

3. See Eugene H. Peterson, *The Message* (Colorado Springs: NavPress, 2002).

4. *Merriam-Webster's Collegiate Dictionary*, 11th ed., (2003) s.v. "joy."

5. The Greek words translated "joy" and "grace" are *chara* and *charis*, respectively.

6. Richard Foster, *Prayer: Finding the Heart's True Home* (San Francisco: HarperSanFrancisco, 1992), 84.

7. F.F. Bruce, *Philippians*, New International Biblical Commentary (Peabody, MA: Hendrickson Publishers, 1990), 142.

8. Joseph M. Scriven, "What a Friend We Have in Jesus" (1855).

9. Bruce, *Philippians*, 144.

10. Bruce, *Philippians*, 145.

11. See the discussion in Bruce, *Philippians*, 145-6.

12. Bruce, *Philippians*, 146.

CHAPTER 6

1. William Law, *An Affectionate Address to the Clergy* [1761]; republished as *The Power of the Spirit*, edited by Dave Hunt (Fort Washington, PA: Christian Literature Crusade, 1993; originally published, 1971), 44-45.

2. Francis MacNutt, *Healing*, 40.

3. Wayne Grudem, *Systematic Theology* (Grand Rapids, MI: Zondervan, 1994), 1016. For more information on the theology of the Holy Spirit and the historical practice of spiritual gifts, see Max Turner, *The Holy Spirit and Spiritual Gifts* (Peabody, MA: Hendrickson Publishers, 1998; originally published: Carlisle, U.K.: Paternoster Press, 1996). The book is a scholarly yet readable work of New Testament criticism and historical theology. See also J. Rodman Williams, *Renewal Theology*, vol. 2 (Grand Rapids, MI: Zondervan, 1990), Chapter 14.

4. C. Peter Wagner, *Your Spiritual Gifts Can Help Your Church Grow* (Ventura, CA: Regal Books, 1994), 34.

5. Grudem, *Systematic Theology*, 1018.

6. For definitions of various spiritual gifts mentioned in the Bible, see Wagner, *Your Spiritual Gifts Can Help Your Church Grow.*

7. See Dennis and Rita Bennett, *The Holy Spirit and You* (Plainfield, NJ: Logos International, 1971), 83. The Bennetts categorize spiritual gifts as 1) gifts of knowledge, 2) gifts of speech, and 3) gifts of power.

8. For some of the technical information in this section, I am indebted to the following commentaries: James B. Adamson, *The Epistles of James*, The New International Commentary on the New Testament, ed. F.F. Bruce (Grand Rapids, MI: William B. Eerdmans Publishing Company, 1976); Peter H. Davids, *James*, New International Biblical Commentary (Peabody, MA: Hendrickson Publishers, 1993); and Douglas J. Moo, *James*, Tyndale New Testament Commentaries (Grand Rapids, MI: William B. Eerdmans Publishing Company, 1990; originally published, 1985).

9. We all will face death should the Lord delay His coming (see Heb. 9:27). No one whom Jesus and the disciples healed in their earthly ministries is now alive. Physical healing is only a temporary and partial provision until the return of Jesus Christ for His Church. Physical healing is a foretaste of a future reality in which we will have everlasting, incorruptible bodies. When it is time for each of us to face death, we can do so with dignity because God loves us and He will raise us up again at the resurrection from the dead.

10. The Christian doctor Reginald Cherry discusses the medical and spiritual sides of physical healing in Reginald Cherry, M.D., *Healing Prayer: God's Divine Intervention in Medicine, Faith, and Prayer* (Nashville, TN: Thomas Nelson, 1999). He states, "God uses doctors, medicines, herbs, nutrition, supplements, exercise, prayer, and miraculous interventions of all kinds to heal us. But He wants to heal us, and He will" (120-21).

11. In his journal entries for March 17, 1746; September 2, 1781; and May 23, 1783, John Wesley recounts several incidents of the recovery of his horses from lameness through prayer. See John Wesley, *Journal*, in *The Works of John Wesley*, 14 vols. (Grand Rapids, MI: Baker, 1996), 4:216, 4:247.

CHAPTER 7

1 Francis Schaeffer, *Death in the City* (Downers Grove, IL: InterVarsity Press, 1969), 134.

2. John Wimber, "Zip to 3,000 in Five Years," in C. Peter Wagner, ed., *Signs and Wonders Today: The Story of Fuller Theological Seminary's Remarkable Course on Spiritual Power* (Altamonte Springs, FL: Creation House, 1987), 34.

3. Unless otherwise noted, all Scripture references in this chapter will be from the NKJV.

4. See Henry J. Cadbury, ed., *George Fox's 'Book of Miracles'* (Quakers United in Publishing, 2000; Cambridge: Cambridge University Press, 1948; reprinted, 1973). The book has around 150 accounts of the supernatural.

5. John Wesley, *Journal* [December 26, 1761], in *The Works of John Wesley*, 12 vols. (Grand Rapids, MI: Baker, 1996), 3:76-77.

6. Wesley, *Journal* [April 12, 1784], in *Works*, 4:270.

7. See Wilfred Graves, "Popular and Elite Understandings of Miracles in Enlightened England" (Ph.D. dissertation, Fuller Theological Seminary, 2007).

8. Gloria and William J. Gaither, "There's Something about that Name" (1970).

9. Eddie Carswell and Babbie Mason, "Trust His Heart" (Dayspring Music (BMI) / May Sun Music / Word Music, 1989).

CHAPTER 8

1. Oswald Chambers, *My Utmost for His Highest: An Updated Edition in Today's Language*, edited by James Reimann (Grand Rapids, MI: Discovery House Publishers, 1992), entry for August 28.

2. Unless otherwise indicated, all Scripture references in this chapter are from the NKJV.

3. John R. Stott, *The Letters of John*, rev. ed. Tyndale New Testament Commentaries (Grand Rapids, MI: William B. Eerdmans Publishing Company, 1988), 188.

4. I.H. Marshall, *The Epistles of John*, New International Commentary (Grand Rapids, MI: Eerdmans, 1978), 245.

CHAPTER 9

1. J.D. Watson, *The Word for the Day,* AMG Publishers, 2006.

2. Oswald Chambers, *My Utmost for His Highest,* Discovery House Publishers, 2008.

3. The acronym S.M.A.R.T. comes from the world of project management. Its origin is unknown.

CHAPTER 10

1. Do not misunderstand verses such as Second Chronicles
   16:12. The Bible here does not condemn the medical pro-
   fession. Asa, in an act of unbelief and disobedience, refused to seek the Lord for healing and opted only for the
   earthly wisdom of physicians, who presumably did not
   honor God in their practice.

Appendix A

Questions and Answers About Salvation and Wholeness

Questions

1. If God is good, then why does so much bad happen in the world?

2. Do salvation and wholeness come through Jesus Christ alone?

3. How can I receive salvation?

4. How can I know whether my life is pleasing to God?

5. Are demons involved in mental illness?

6. What advice can I give to someone who is struggling to forgive?

7. Why do some people not receive miraculous healing when they pray?

8. Did miracles cease with the death of the last apostle?

9. What comfort can I give to someone suffering from a chronic illness?

10. Is it possible not to commit sin?

11. How can I operate in spiritual gifts?

12. If God is in control of everything, then why do I need to pray?

13. Is the Bible relevant for today?

14. Am I worthy enough to minister wholeness to others?

15. Can anything good come from suffering?

Question 1:
If God is good, then why does so much bad happen in the world?

God is good. He is the source of all that makes life possible and meaningful. Evil entered into the world because of human choices. God's remedy for evil is salvation, which He offers to humanity through His Son, Jesus Christ. Salvation is a process that unfolds in human history. It takes time for human beings to learn, to mature, and to grow. God ultimately will destroy evil and its effects when His redemptive process is complete. Until that time, He will sustain His people with His presence, power, and provisions.

Question 2:
Do salvation and wholeness come through Jesus Christ alone?

Jesus describes Himself as *"the way, the truth, and the life"* in John 14:6 (NKJV). The apostle Paul states in Acts 4:12 that we can find salvation in none else but Jesus Christ. Jesus Christ gives us access to the blessings and provisions of God. He alone is the true source of salvation and wholeness.

Question 3:
How can I receive salvation?

Read Romans 10:9-10. Salvation comes through the acceptance of Jesus' work on the cross, the belief in His resurrection from the dead, and the embrace of His Lordship over one's life.

Question 4:
How can I know whether my life is pleasing to God?

If Jesus Christ is your Lord and Savior, then you are in right relationship with God. A life that is in right relationship with God will also evidence spiritual fruit, such as love, joy, peace, etc. Obedience is also a requirement for pleasing God. Each day, God's children should seek Him in prayer, meditate on His Word, and humbly walk in the truth that they know. A heart that is sensitive and open to God is pleasing to Him.

Question 5:
Are demons involved in mental illness?

Demons sometimes can be involved in physical or mental illness. To detect them will require a spiritual gift of discernment unless their presence is obvious from observation. Jesus Christ is the name (or authority) by which we subjugate evil forces. Command them to leave. Not all mental illness is the result of demonic activity, though. Some mental illnesses require medication and professional diagnosis.

Question 6:
What advice can I give to someone who is struggling to forgive?

Do not dismiss the person's pain too quickly. Listen to and empathize with him or her. Pray with the person and ask God to reveal Himself to the person in a special way. Try to help the person to realize that there is healing in forgiveness. Allow the person to pray for the one who committed the offense. Sometimes great freedom can result from such a selfless act.

Question 7:
Why do some people not receive miraculous healing when they pray?

Miraculous healing is only one of many ways that God works. God works through doctors, through diet and exercise, through consistent prayer, and through a plethora of other ways. He heals instantly, progressively, or in manners that are somewhat different from what we may expect. God wants us to trust Him and to seek His wisdom so that we can find our individual pathway to wholeness. Even if God does not heal us in the way that we would choose, His choice will be what is best for us.

Question 8:
Did miracles cease with the death of the last apostle?

No. The Bible never claims a cessation of miracles. The testimony of the Church throughout history also attests to the continuation of God's miracle-working power.

Question 9:
What comfort can I give to someone suffering from a chronic illness?

The best comfort is a reassurance of the love and presence of God. Love itself has healing effects. When we show love to others, our actions reveal the love of God to them. Please see Appendix B.

Question: 10:
Is it possible not to commit sin?

Everyone commits sins or individual acts of wrongdoing; however, Christ frees us from the power of sin or alienation from God. Because the Lord has dealt with the sin problem, we do not have to commit sin. We are not slaves to sin, and we can experience victory over sin continually.

Question 11:
How can I operate in spiritual gifts?

If you have received salvation, then you are ready to yield to the Holy Spirit for direction and empowerment. Ask the Lord to fill you with the Holy Spirit, and present yourself to Him for service to other people. As you begin to operate in a spirit of love and open yourself to God's wisdom, voice, and power, the gifts of the Spirit will emerge.

Question 12:
If God is in control of everything, then why do I need to pray?

Prayer is one way that God chooses to exercise His power on earth. He does not need us in an absolute sense, but He does allow us to participate with Him to advance His Kingdom. Furthermore, prayer is a worship activity in which our fellowship with God deepens and grows.

Question 13:
Is the Bible relevant for today?

Yes! The Bible is the written Word of God. The Bible is relevant because God certainly is relevant.

Question 14:
Am I worthy enough to minister wholeness to others?

Jesus Christ makes you worthy. God uses ordinary people to do extraordinary things.

Question 15:
Can anything good come from suffering?

Suffering is not good in itself; however, God can cause all things to work together for good (see Rom. 8:28). Sometimes

God's people will endure trials and hardships in order to learn perseverance or to grow into maturity (see James 1:2-4). If we are enduring trials, we should seek God's wisdom and direction in them (see James 1:5-8). If others are enduring trials, we should provide them with prayerful support and an understanding ear, without platitudes, simplistic clichés, rebuking them for lack of faith, defending God's actions, or telling them our opinions as to why they are suffering. No one wants to suffer and to hear our explanations of why he or she is suffering.

Trusting God in Difficult Times

We all have difficult times in our lives. Sometimes our prayers go unanswered for significant periods. Sometimes we cannot discern God's activity in certain situations. There are other times when our trust in God has not failed, but the situation nonetheless is just plain difficult. Imagine how Abraham felt when God told him at the age of 75 that he would have a son, and 25 years later Isaac was born (see Gen. 12:1-4; 21:1-5). What about Joseph, who, 13 years after his dream of exaltation, found himself in an Egyptian prison (see Gen. 37:2; 41:46)? The woman with the issue of blood suffered for 12 years before receiving a miracle (see Mark 5:25-34). Luke writes of a woman with a spirit of infirmity that crippled her for 18 years before she was healed (see Luke 13:11-13). The man at the pool of Bethesda waited for 38 years before he encountered the Lord Jesus Christ (see John 5:5-9). Sometimes the trials in our lives last for quite a while.

Job's ordeal is a classic Old Testament example of suffering. Job is a prosperous man, whom God describes as blameless and upright (e.g., see Job 1:1,8). After a satanic assault, Job loses everything that he has. His friends are of little comfort and try to convince him that he has sinned. Job, of course, is hurting and bewildered, so he questions God (see Job 23:1-7ff.). Job's questions do not offend God, but God does pose some questions of His own (see Job 38–41).

God never really answers any of Job's questions; He simply reveals to Job how great He is as the Creator. The lesson here is that God is greater than any trial or difficulty we may face. We should take our eyes off our problems and put them on God. God is challenging Job to grow in faith. God answers Job, not with intellectual explanations, but rather with His presence. Job responds in 42:1-6 that he has a clearer understanding of the ways of the Lord. He is able to see the love and goodness of God apart from his life situation. The story of Job ends with restoration; God gives Job twice what he had before (see Job 42:12-17).

Although sin often brings difficulties into our lives, these experiences do not necessarily mean that we have committed a sin. Many of the heroes of the Christian faith suffered or even died because of their devotion to God (e.g., see Heb. 11). God sometimes allows us to confront challenges because it helps others to see His power at work in our lives. At other times, God tests us in order to bring us to a point of maturity. Trials and hardships can produce perseverance, humility, and other Christian character traits. Although God is not the source of evil and suffering, He sometimes works through human difficulties to accomplish His own holy purposes. Romans 8:28 assures us, *"In all things God works for the good of those who love Him, who have been called according to His purpose."*

Sometimes God says no to our requests. Paul experienced such a response from God concerning his *"thorn in my flesh"* (2 Cor. 12:7-10). Jesus Christ Himself faced "unanswered prayer" as He agonized in the Garden of Gethsemane (see Luke 22:39-46). Sometimes God has a purpose that is greater than the results that we are seeking. Rest assured, though, that if God says no, then His answer is best. God does not say no simply because He can do so. He says no because the answer will lead to the best outcome for us. Although we will not always understand God's actions, we do know that He is with us and that He loves us.

Difficult times are easier to face when we keep a clear account with God. Many things can hinder our prayers and progress in the Christian life. Some of these include sin, wavering faith, wrong motives, marital conflict, and unforgiveness. Some of the things for which we pray are worldly, silly, or out of the will of God. We need to seek God diligently for His wisdom during our prayer times.

When we find ourselves in difficult times, we need to remind ourselves that God is with us; He is right there to sustain us. Yet, we must not confuse the presence of God with the warm feelings that often accompany His presence. God is with us whether we sense His presence or not. He also monitors and controls the trials that we face, and ultimately, He will work out everything for our good. God loves us and is on our side. He wants to give us joy, peace, strength, and the things that we need to accomplish His will and purposes in our lives.

When we pray, we should ask God for wisdom, repent of known sins, and meditate on the Word of God. It is usually helpful to reflect on what God has done for us in the past. As we do this, we gain assurance that He will come through for us in the present. In our prayer times, we should recall God's last instructions to us. If we have not yet obeyed these instructions, then we need to take steps to do so. If we have obeyed His instructions, then we can wait for new ones. If we do not discern new instructions from God, then we cautiously should make informed choices based on the knowledge that we have from the Word and other godly counsel.

It is extremely important that we do not allow trials to "crowd out" the full range of God's dealings with us. Our problems, deficiencies, weaknesses, and trials do not define us. God has more for us, so we should wait on Him with expectation. Even during times of great perplexity, we can always worship the Lord. We can always magnify His name. Finally, we must not forget to bring others into our times of difficulty. God never intended the Christian journey to be a lonely one. We need other people to pray for us and to support us.

About Dr. Wilfred Graves Jr.

Wilfred Graves Jr. is the only child of Wilfred and Glendolyn Graves. He was born in New Orleans, Louisiana, and raised in Columbus, Georgia. A high school valedictorian, he received a full scholarship to Massachusetts Institute of Technology, where he majored in mathematics and graduated as a top-ten student in the discipline. After graduating from MIT, he went on to receive a master of science in Statistics from Stanford University, a master of divinity from Fuller Theological Seminary, and a Ph.D. in historical theology from Fuller Seminary. The title of his doctoral dissertation was "Popular and Elite Understandings of Miracles in Enlightened England." He also worked as an aerospace engineer for five years.

Dr. Graves made a commitment to the Lord Jesus Christ during early childhood, and acknowledged the call to ministry in his mid-teens. He has been involved in public ministry since 1988 and was ordained in 1999. He currently serves West Angeles Church of God in Christ as executive coordinator. He assists the senior pastor with the daily ministry of the church and with various local, national, and international projects. He also oversees the development and training of the church's licensed and ordained clergy.

Dr. Graves teaches courses at West Angeles Bible College and has taught as an adjunct instructor at Fuller Theological Seminary.

IN THE RIGHT HANDS, THIS BOOK WILL CHANGE LIVES!

Most of the people who need this message will not be looking for this book. To change their lives, you need to put a copy of this book in their hands.

> *But others (seeds) fell into good ground, and brought forth fruit, some a hundred-fold, some sixty-fold, some thirty-fold* (Matthew 13:8).

Our ministry is constantly seeking methods to find the good ground, the people who need this anointed message to change their lives. Will you help us reach these people?

> *Remember this—a farmer who plants only a few seeds will get a small crop. But the one who plants generously will get a generous crop* (2 Corinthians 9:6).

EXTEND THIS MINISTRY BY SOWING
3 BOOKS, 5 BOOKS, 10 BOOKS, OR MORE TODAY,
AND BECOME A LIFE CHANGER!

Thank you,

Don Nori Sr., Publisher
Destiny Image
Since 1982

Made in the USA
Middletown, DE
26 April 2021